T0078129

HELL AND BACK

OPTIMUM VIZHAN

www.trafford.com
North America & international
toll-free: 844-688-6899 (USA & Canada)
fax: 812 355 4082

Contents

✝ Dedication ✝

This book is dedicated to
All the Service Men and Women
who did not and will not
get the chance to enjoy a life companion,
children, grand children and etc;
for the rest of their lives,
due to their passing while
serving their country.
And to those who have lost Love Ones,
Hoping to Share Your Lives with Them
for the Rest of Your lives;
Only to hear the News,
that Your Loved One
has Passed on While Serving
Their Country...

Here's
Sobering Moment of Silence
to Honor You...

Now God's Compassion
and Strength Preserve
You Forever.

God Bless You
and Your Loved Ones...
forever and ever!

Author

✝ Dedication II ✝

This book is dedicated to My Wife
for Never Giving up on Us:
as a couple, as a family and as an
Inspiration to others;
to help them face their hell.

I also want to...

My first son;
for Allowing Me to Live and Die
the Way I want to ...
for Writing This Book for Me
About My life.

I Chose to Love You All by My Actions;
for they will and did speak louder than words
could ever speak.

God Bless My Family
and the families they have
forever and ever.

Richard

✝ Habakkuk ✝

Then the LORD replied:
"Write down the revelation
and make it plain on tablets
so that a herald may run with it.
For the revelation awaits
an appointed time;
it speaks of its manifestation
and will prove not self-centered.
Though it lingers,
wait for it;
it will certainly come
and will not delay.

Habakkuk 2:2-3
New Friendship
Bible

✝ Disclaimer ✝

S on: This is an unedited manuscript. This book is written in an interview diary type format, based on what dad remembers, on a select number of events that took place in his life. Most of this book is written based on what he and I personally experienced. I will add more details to his events based on: what I personally experienced with him and from the countless times he told these stories to me. And a cumulative perspective based on an overview of everything woven together and the reoccurring patterns of God establishing his life to be an inspiration to others.

Son: Going through his wife's belongings after she passed; he found a note pad with what appears to be the beginning of her memoirs. She began with her childhood and then how she met him. What's all the more intriguing is she started writing her memoirs on 08-08-2008. We will be including her complete memoir as a separate chapter.

Son: We also found dad's mother in law's memoirs that she dictated to mom, about their family's life before, during and after the Great Depression; in the Flint Michigan and the neighboring cities. We will be adding her memoirs in a separate chapter as well. However, her memoirs have a lot more details so we will be gleaning out the references that lead up to how dad met mom as teenagers.

Son: Any scripture references listed will be from the New Friendship Bible, less otherwise stated.

✝ Preface ✝

S on: Dad would joke from time to time about writing his memoirs someday. Those days did pass by too quickly. He and I have decided it's time to write his life story. Thinking too, it was a good past time hanging out with each other, while going through our Michigan Winter. Then come out of our man caves with a published book about his life story. Awesome, let's do it.

Dad: I was in Two Wars; One with Korea and one with My Wife.

Son: In both, dad had to learn to come at peace with himself and God. This would allow him to focus on facing his hells head on and witnessing God walking him through them at the same time; establishing him again with new resources that would take him through the next season of his life.

Son: Dad's life started at the end of the Great Depression in the 20th Century, on his father's large self-sustaining farm. His dad's large farm supported the needs of his family, those who lived in the local communities and those who drove a few hours for his hard cider and meats.

Son: His father's home was a big farm house, built for a big family; two stories, two stairs one each end of the house going to the upstairs, gas lights, full walk in pantry, big wood burning pot belly fire furnace between the living room and dining room, big wood burning stove for cooking for the family and hired hands, cellar, front and east side full wrap around porches. Lots of windows, his sisters had one big window in their room. His mom and dad had a big bedroom down stairs with its own stair way to the upstairs.

Son: Two barns; one large barn that held the large livestock: cows, horses, etc and the smaller barn held the smaller livestock: chickens, goats, etc.

Son: Dad believes his dad or grandpa planted an Apple Orchard when he/they was/were younger, from which he sold apples, hard and sweet ciders. His mom grew gardens that provided vegetables for the family and the local communities. While his siblings took turns milking the cows for milk, cream, cottage cheese and his favorite - ice cream.

Son: A creek ran through the farm and a small pond just east of the farm house, up by the road.

Son: Dad had seven siblings before he was born; one sister and six brothers; all a few years apart from each other.

Son: Gypsies with covered wagons full of goods to sell would go by the farm, on regular bases. If they or others didn't have a place to sleep at night, his dad would let them sleep in the barn with the animals.

Son: Looking back I can see the season's dad's life went through. From the day he was born to the day the family buck sheep rammed him into the steel wheel on the tractor. From the buck sheep ramming him into the steel wheel to the day he met his life long sweet heart. From the day he met his sweet heart to his flower shop. From the day he started his flower shop to being drafted into the Korean War. From the day he was drafted into the Korean War to his marriage. From the day he was married to returning from the Korean War. From the day he returned from the Korean War to the farm house. From the day he moved into the farm house to his sister-in-laws. From the day he moved into his sister-n-laws to his flint home. From the day he moved into his flint home to he's wife's passing. From the day his wife passed on to the publishing of his life story. From the day he's life story was officially published to who knows what at this moment in his life. They would all start with God setting him up and then end it with someone trying to set him back.

Son: The purpose in writing dad's memoirs is to inspire people not to give up on their lives, when they find themselves facing their own hell; to relax, wait upon God and let Him show them a way out. Be it near death experiences; on the farm, in war, driving vehicles, building homes, marriage, heart attack, a bypass and lost of a loved one.

Dad: Ok. Enough of the commercials, let's get started.

✝ The Day I was Born ✝

Dad: Mom had my twin sister first while lying on the dining room thick oak table. After she was born, dad and the doctor went to drinking hard cider, shooting the breeze. Mom started moving on table. Doc said, I think there's another up there? Stopped drinking so they delivered me. It was more like a celebration, happy for twins. Had seven children; me and my twin sister made nine.

Son: Did the old doc get drunk?

Dad: He sure did like the hard cider. Big farm house; seven to nine rooms upstairs.

Son: Dad was you glad you were born in Michigan?

Dad: Yes.

Son: Why?

Dad: I had no choice.

✝ Family Pet Sheep ✝

D ad: Nice day. Playing outside by the buck sheep, he was our play mate; the family pet. Healthy, strong. He would butt me around. He butted me into the tractor wheel. Happen so fast, I didn't have time. It had steel wheels with "V" welded on the wheel for traction. It left a "V" scar on my head. "V" for victory. I beat for once.

Dad: My dad grabs him in one hand. Butcher knife; cut his head right off, one swipe. Dad killed his prized buck sheep.

Son: My dad would mention that his dad never talked much; he would never hug him or say he loved him. Man, of action.

Dad: Looking back I know now my dad loved me because he didn't think twice in killing his well praised prized buck sheep.

Son: My dad's eyes would water up sometimes after telling this story. The buck sheep weighted about 200 lbs. His dad lifted him up with one hand and with a butcher knife cut his head off with the other. No hesitation.

Dad: The buck sheep would play in the yard like a regular pet dog would. Families have dogs as pets; we had a buck sheep as a family pet.

Son: Dad, you remember how old you were?

Dad: I was three, not over five.

Son: It's like the sheep knew it was born for this purpose of imprinting the "V" scar on my father's head, so that dad would always know God would be with him and get him through his life's head-butting challenges. That moment, the buck sheep's eyes peacefully looked into my father's eyes, like any good pet would do; to show their appreciation of their human bond. It's like the sheep calculated the space, my father's position and the force needed to ram my father's body/head into the "V" welded part of the tractor wheel, so that the "V" would appear on the front of my dad's head; off to the upper left side. My dad had a full set of hair with a widow's pattern baldness taking shape over the years. So, at first the "V" was hidden in his locks. As dad grew older and the more head-butting challenges he had, the "V" scar would be revealed/easier to see. At first glance, it can't be seen but looking closer at dad's forehead, you can see the clear "V" shaped scar on his forehead. It also like the buck sheep knew that his contribution to dad's life story was to be the sacrificial ram; to cover dad's life. That his blood was shed, so that dad's life would be spared in all those darkest moments of his life.

Son: Before rubber tires were invented, the tractors wheels were made out of solid steel, with "V" shape patterns welded on the steel wheel so that the tractor would get traction while driving. It's like the "V" scar on dad's forehead would give him traction while driving through the hells he would find himself in over the years.

Son: His dad was overseeing everything on his farm; the crops, the hired hands, the orchard, the farm animals, his eight other children and his faithful wife, who stood by him even when he got drunk. By his in a twinkling of an eye response, he must have been keeping a closer distance and eye on his newest son, playing with the family pet sheep. Him being a man of few words; didn't call out warnings of being careful. He let his son make choices and take chances with the possibility of confronting the deadly muscle force of a 200 lb buck sheep. It was more like his dad was on a standby execution; hoping not to be the one who takes the family pet's life and or feeling ashamed of himself, for trusting the family pet wouldn't take his twin son's life. Either way, the next few moments would clarify to all those who were watching and to those who would be hearing to what just happen, for the first time. How a little boys' life was saved. How the bloody scar was marked on his forehead and the act of love that saved his life. Seeing his special birthed son knocked out cold at the foot of his tractor's back wheel, while fearing his son's bloody head wasn't a sign of his son's death. He welded all of his strength, lifted his prized sheep in the air with one arm; looked in the eyes of his pet. Regretting his decision of not shouting warnings; that could have avoided this moment. Then turning to see what appeared his special son's short life span and holding the butcher knife so hard that felt like it was an extension of his hand; he took the life of his family's trusted pet. His father's adrenaline rush dissipates into an ashamed, helpless, humbling arms cradling his knocked-out son; while asking for God's mercy quietly in his heart.

✝ My Dad ✝

Dad: My dad was a big man six feet one or two inches. He had big hands, big ears, big nose. He loved his hard cider he made himself, beer, Redman chewing tobacco. Spit six feet, in the house; would spit in stove.

Dad: He would line up brothers and sisters everyday and whip them if needed or not; except for me and Maxine. If he was going to whip you, he was going to whip you. When he talked he meant it. He was strict.

Dad: He cut off his ear while shaving, put it back on, bandage it and it grew back on a little crooked.

Son: Back then, men shaved with a metal blade that they would keep sharp by wiping it back and forth on each side of the blade's edge, rather hard and quick on a three to four-inch-wide piece of leather.

Dad: Rod Smith, bachelor, lived on the farm. Picked apples; hired hand. He must be a hundred years old now. It's been so damn long ago, I forgot myself.

Son: Dad would mention over the years, most ever time his dad would go into town; he would trade with everyone sitting at the local bar front counter. He would go from one end to the other; bartering what he had on his farm with others what he needed for his family, himself and the farm. When he got done, he would get drunk and start a fight. When he gets drunk, he wanted to fight. The guys would pile on him to hold him down but they all couldn't do it. He loved it. He loved people. He loved interacting with them with his actions.

Son: Dad would say his dad had one tooth and joked around that he used it to open beer bottles.

Son: Dad would mention that his dad only had a 2nd grade education. The thought as to why; be his dad was a farmer; all he needed to know was how to farm. From his 2nd grade education and his farming experience, he knew enough to make sure his family had income coming in every month with Cows, Chickens, Sheep, Gardens, Apple Orchard, Farm Field Crops. Plus acquiring 200 plus acres; with no debt and nine children.

✝ My Childhood ✝

D ad: Born in Depression. Growing up into good times.
Dad: Things are changing. Farmers did good in Great
Depression; had basic needs take care of

Dad: Bank didn't make my dad make payments because of
his big family. Better to occupy house then abandon it.

Dad: Dad wasted no time in whipping us. He use his two
inch shaving razor leather strap to whip us.

Dad: Skated with twin sister on pond, using one skate each,
from the same pair of skates. Holded each other and skated
as one person.

Dad: Milk cows' night and day. Put milk in cooler. Four by
eight-foot cooler. Hold eight cans of milk.

Dad: Make ice-cream all the time. Made ourselves. Eight-
quart freezer. Jersey cow milk. Holstein cows didn't have
much crème in milk. In winter ice came from pond. Buy
blocks of ice in the summer time. Smashed it up. Stored in
the ground; dug a hole.

Dad: Wrestle as kids. Four against five. Nobody wins. All
about the same. Fight a lot; dragged it out.

Dad: While riding with my brother in car, car hit ridge in
road and flipped the car over. Neighbor came out to see if
we were ok and asked if we needed any toilet paper.

Dad: Two brothers hung together. Close. One heavy set. Neither married. Jersey cows fifty percent crème. Big cows big tits. Turn that tit on the cow on them and squirted him in face really hard. Shot milk eight feet. Scored in his face. Splattered him. Throwed that milk like ten to twelve feet. I would run right away from him. He chased me out of the barn, in the field and half way to the woods. The field had wheat stubble sheaves. It was before we had a combine. Couldn't catch me. Must weighed 280lbs. He would have to sit to rest. He would come over just to watch us milk cows. As much as they come down to watch us milk, you would think they would want to help us but didn't. Always come back afterwards, that was their entertainment. Made fun out of it; had fun growing up.

Dad: My twin sister and I would help mom plant big garden. Half to acre garden. All of cousins came over to do canning to fill pantry up; sixteen foot by eight foot. Enough food for all winter. Can three to four days straight. Little pickles would be more money. Grew pickles and used them to buy groceries.

Dad: Made a lot of pies, make a dozen pies. We would try to sneak them. Favorite pie is cherry. Raised fruit for that; apples and cherries.

Dad: Caught house on fire upstairs. My twin sister and I went into the girl's room. One room together at end of house. Ages five or six. Playing with matches. Tried to light them in closet. Had a box of matches. Had to light fires with matches. Didn't do anything but watch it burn. Sit by fire. One neighbor had the only phone around. They called fire department. Fire department came fast. Had out in no time; only burnt window out of girl's room. No whipping. Sense of adventure. The whole floor should have blown up from the gas going to the gas lamps.

Dad: One of my older brothers had a rifle, shot at a bird on the roof of barn. So dad took the gun away from my brother and busted it over cast iron kettle; busted a chunk out of the kettle. Made dad so mad because he shot into the barn to get the bird – barn full of animals their lively hood; he took about six inches out of rim of kettle.

Dad: I got a whipping between ten to fifteen years old. It hurt. Bend over. It stinged. Dad would whip us until we cried. You knew when got into trouble you knew you got ass whipped. His hand was twice as big as mine.

Dad. Ice pond front right of house next to the road. Some times the school kids would come out and skate on it. Hard time to get us off pond to go eat. We all loved to skate.

Dad: My Dad butchered bulls, pigs, sheep; mainly hogs and bulls. Lots of chickens. Butcher once a week. Feed them grain to get a lot of beef, regular beef bulls. Take the guts and body parts back in the fields and bury.

Dad: One of my brothers and I worked with cows, not much pork.

Dad: House big basement; kept cider, made our own cream from Jersey cow.

Dad: People coming up from Detroit, neighboring cities to get hard cider, sweet cider and butchered a cow for them

Dad: One radio. We all sat around and listened to it. Had to run a long copper wire from house to barn about hundred feet. Favorite show to listen to is Long Ranger and Tonto. Dad listened to news in mornings.

Dad: One out house for eleven people. Cleaned out every week. Spread around in field. Older boys. Three seats, big one, middle one and small one. Took turns using.

Sometimes two. Tipped over when someone was in there. Four or five boys try to tip over. Gang up against. For entertainment.

Dad: Winter months open up a window and pee out window. The window would be bleach by summer. Yellow ice cycles. Boys window over porch roof.

Dad: Water pump in kitchen. Had to prime it. Leather seal had to be wet. Cooked hot water on stove. Bathed in tub by the stove by the door. Four by eight; one a week if needed it or not.

Dad: Boys slept together; girls by themselves.

Dad: Smoked corn silk. In the fall when corn silk turns brown. Pull over the ear. Rolled it by itself. Smoked it behind the barn. Thought was cool smoking it.

Dad: Long cigs first. Six cents each. Smoked off and on but no effort to smoking. Done a little bit; had to be careful not to catch stuff on fire.

Dad: A lot of snow ball fights. Spare off.

Dad: Elevator to cider press had a grinder. Heavy cheese cloth in racks between them. Hydraulic press. Person on each side, racks about two four inches deep. I was about ten when started helping make cider. Make once a week sometimes twice for the neighbors.

Dad: Seven boys had the rest of the house. My older brother got married and they had one room in dad's farm house for a couple of years. They cleaned up made livable; the other end of house (opposite of girl's room). Dad didn't like my brother's wife's folks. Real strict.

Dad: I was coming up from the Orchard one day. Dad said, I wasn't going to amount too much, won't have a pot to piss in. I stopped. Looked him in the eye and said, "One of these days I'm going to buy you out and have a gold seat on my toilet"

Dad: People would say to my dad that the devil is going to get him. Dad would say, "I ain't afraid of the devil."

☦ Mile And a Half to School ☦

D ad: Summer time. Nice weather, walk to school every day. Wait for the Dayful children. When they come by, we knew it was time for school.

Dad: Went to school no matter how high the snow was. Older brothers would carry me to school. Carry kindergarteners on their shoulders. One room school. The School Teacher had to walk to school as well. I liked kinder garden, not much to do. Country School gave you a lot of free time.

Son: What was your favorite subject?

Dad: Can't remember my favorite subject. I don't think I liked school. I liked recess. One in the morning and one in the afternoon. Played catch, tag; take sides, at least twenty kids.

Dad: My older brother trapped skunk, mink, weasel, sold fur; bought a lot. He was the trapper. The neighbors had big family; they trapped half the river; we trapped the other half. Where the balls are is where the oil was. Skunk oil was good for colds. Put in container. Natural thing to get into trouble. Played tricks on girls. Only recreation we had. We threw the skunk oil into the furnace; stunk up the whole school; sent everyone home. A school friend like to trick too; hung together.

Dad: One of brothers volunteered to go to school early to get school warmed up and kept furnace full of wood. He didn't want to do it one winter, gave to other school kid, so he could take a break. The kid caught school on fire. Hell of a fire, stocked up big boiler. Teacher thought all out but one short. Didn't know where he was. One kid ran back in to the closet, had to climb out. Put out before fire dept got there. Fire department couldn't get there fast enough. Our country school had to consolidate with a neighboring city school, quit the city school after eight grade.

Son: My guess would be Dad's favorite subject was Math. He was quick with adding his numbers in his head. I remember most any time numbers came up in a conversation; he would have the total within seconds. I would take the time to check it and sure enough he was right and or really really close.

✝ My Free Movie Sweet Heart ✝

D ad: She was thirteen, I was sixteen.
Dad: My dad had buddies in the local towns. Summer drove the truck, winter not so much.

Dad: The local town our family like to go to played Free Movies outside, on a screen, summer months only. Us kids would pile in back of dad's ford truck. Dad went to the bar. Kids went to the movie. Mom would buy the groceries.

Dad: We would get pop and ice cream before the movies. Sit on bleachers, at least fifty kids.

Dad: The bar, grocery store and drug store. Went to all the free movies from day one. Favorite Long Ranger and Tonto, mostly cowboy movies, lasted about one and half to two hours. Friendly farm neighborhood so would meet up.

Son: Other than the movies being free, why did you want to see them?

Dad: Just wanted to watch movie with family. Walking; going to our places we normally set; Sally was ahead of me. One look at her that was it.

Son: What attracted you to her?

Dad: Well built. Frisky. Independent. I'm going to hang on her. She stopped to get her place, then me with my family. Offered to get ice cream before movie. The gas station had half of the building as ice-cream parlor. No place to sit, had to sit together. We were satisfied with each other in everything we did. We went along with each other.

Dad: Her dad said, if I harm her, he was going to hang me by the chain fall hanging that was hanging in his tree. He said it like he meant it. It didn't scare me.

Son: After meeting for the first time, what did you two do afterwards?

Dade: Free movies all the time after we met. Every week do something. Movie, Dancing. My older brother would let me use his car.

Dad: I had to milk cows by six am and by six pm. I didn't want to milk cows, so I slowly let them run dry so I could spend more time with my free movie sweet heart.

Dad: I liked flowers more than farming. I plant gladiolas bulbs in banks of the creek that ran through dad's farm. Sell any where for seventy-five cents a dozen. I sold flowers and picked apples for spending money on my sweet heart.

Son: Mom mentioned, she was a tom boy. Her dad wanted a boy so bad; he only had the four girls and her being the last girl, he made/treated as though she was a boy. Take fishing; she baited her own hook, cleaned fish, etc.

Son: Businesses would front the free movies to draw in the people then the people would buy their products since they were there; brilliant marketing.

✝ Dick's Florist ✝

Dad: I quit going to school after the eight grade to help dad on the farm. I didn't like farm work; my dad just let me go. I restored that green house in neighboring town; replaced glass and repaired the boiler. Right time, didn't have to wait for it. I had an operation; vegetables, fruit plant foot high, flowers. Hired ma's sisters; they made it fun.

Dad: Flower shop first year rent free; made most money that year. It took right off. Different people bought vegetables, fruit plants.

Dad: I hired all mom's sisters. They lived southwest of dad's farm, by the Power Dam. Whole bunch of relatives. You would think they take nothing serious. Laughed all the time, fellowship easy; worked hard though. One woman big. Probably weighed 200 lbs. Real active. Home in town, did cooking there. Weekends she took man home. She sure like what she was doing. Get men from the old folk's home. Into her home. Big woman and not afraid of anything. My mother's sister.

Son: Did you have to fire anyone?

Dad: Heavy set man; chewed, smoked cigarettes, fired him. No car, so he started walking to next city.

Son: When dad got drafted into the Korean War, he sold everything that he had in his store, paid off his bills and bought mom an engagement ring with what money he had left.

✝ Getting Married ✝

Dad: My father-in-law was so happy his daughter was marrying me. He liked my dad's family. Her dad wanted her married before I went over to Korea. I think he was going to collect on my insurance if passed.

Dad: Big Wedding day. Married in local town west of Flint; reception at church. Had everything; a lot of cousins on both sides of family.

Dad: He wanted me married. If I got killed he would get the ten thousand. I thought he's not going to get it.

Dad: One relative was always funny, he was never serious, and he was at every party.

Son: Mom was seventeen when she got married, so she had to get her dad's consent. She was still in High School when got married on March 28, 1953. Dad went to Korea shortly afterwards. Dad couldn't remember where they went for their honeymoon, who the best man was and who mom's maid of honor was.

Son: Dad was the only son out of seven sons to leave family for marrying and living a life with his sweet heart, my mom, and to go his own way.

Son: Dad closed down his Flower Shop so that mom wouldn't have to worry about running it while dad was in the Korean War. Dad chose family over wealth.

✝ Korean War ✝

S on: Dad, how did you get to Korea from the States?
Dad: Go by truck, to get to ship. Big passenger boats. Twelve stories high. Took our weapons with us. Drop the rope ladders over ship. I had to climb up with rifle. I had rough time climbing. Ladder was full of guys. I had hard time climbing those rope ladders. I almost lost rifle. A big black guy next to me. Really friendly. He took my rifle put it on his back. He had two rifles on his back. Helped me all the way up. Six foot 2 inches; 200lbs, tough guy. Got rifle from Seattle WA.

Dad: When I got into trouble somebody seemed to be there to help me. That ship was twelve stories high. It was like a city.

Dad: U.S. had a big army and big boats. No problems with boats. They had a good system.

Dad: Got off the shores of Seoul Korea. Went to the front lines. Put a rifle on our shoulders and took us to the front lines.

Dad: It seemed God looked out from me where ever I went. Thank God.

Dad: U.S. had a good plan. Take air planes bomb the hell out of them. When put in a lot of bombing before infantry. The infantry didn't have much to do.

Dad: Thirty-Eight Parallel runs through Bay City, Michigan.

Dad: Two Koreans couldn't get along so split on thirty –eighth parallel, ran through Bay City. Weather same as Michigan.

Dad: North was angry as hell. He didn't give in at all. A lot of hills; big hills, vegetation same.

Dad: The heavy infantry went in first. They had VAR; more like a machine guns. Heavy rifle.

Dad: Light infantry had smaller gun. Every angle of the army. The U.S. was very well equipped. Safer there then on the street.

Dad: Got my false teeth, I had poor teeth, Teeth pulled by short dentist. Would give me a break from front line. I wanted some rest from the front lines so have tooth pulled. Short guy stand on box, move box around every time, he didn't have problem pulling teeth. Go back and forth and bingo. I had poor teeth. Dentist was Korean.

Son: You make any friends while in the army?

Dad: Didn't make any friends, strictly army.

Dad: Three months of actual combat. No hand to hand. Shoot to kill. Fox hole.

Dad: Wrote letters every day I could to my wife. Write all the time. Write down what I was thinking at the time.

Son: Dad said it felt like he spent two years in Korea.

Dad: After war went into bunkers. Settle down.

Dad: Went to Tokyo on R&R; bought twelve-piece China. Settled down. Business all up. All done fighting, they got civilized. I bought China, set of twelve dishes, sent them all home. Still got em. The China got one-eighth gold trim, real gold.

Dad: Shot bullet in corner post. Raising hell. Got so quiet could hear a pin drop. Received metal.

Dad: Took baths in small creek, by river, moved around, set up baths one hundred people take bath at the same time.

Dad: Bathroom out in open, piss tubes. Bazooka shells, five inches. Toilets up two feet up off ground.

Dad; Air raids.

Dad: Rations of Hersey bars and cigarettes. Would trade my cigarettes for Hershey bars.

Son: What were you thinking the night they declared peace?

Dad: It sounded good. Couldn't believe it. We kept guard.

Son: Religious people around you?

Dad: No. Didn't notice. Can't remember.

Son: How did you find out?

Dad: Don't remember.

Dad: Always rifles next to us. Guard change every eight hours to twelve hours. Slept in barracks in sleeping bags.

Son: Snakes?

Dad: Little snake quarter inch by foot; very poisonous. Get behind them, grab their tails; snap the body and snap their heads right off. Dad would do it on the farm. We had gardener snakes, several types here; Korea had the same too.

Dad: Took turns on guard. Good prisoners. Gave us no trouble. They knew they got good food. We was treating them better than their own leaders was.

Dad: Big compounds under barb wire fence. About twelve feet high. On the ground they didn't give us any trouble. They was glad we were there. Looked like they was going to break out we would increase the guards. They never broke out.

Dad: Guard post I was on was a strategic point. Where anything could happen. They rattled the roof boards. I shot into the corner post, six to eight inches thick. It quieted right down. You could hear yourself think.

Dad: They knew better. They were living better in the compound then in their country. Very poor. Good place to sleep.

Dad: You have a M1 in your hand you wasn't afraid of anything. Young.

Dad: Winter is like our weather in Michigan.

Dad: They had no weapons. We had the M1 like a deer rifle. We had clips. We had several clips on us.

Dad: My brother was mechanic in the Air Force. Always on base close to home. Had it easy; lived like kings.

Dad: Army had all the rough stuff. We was young, we could handle it.

Son: Dad would talk about driving a jeep around for a General, after 38th Parallel Peace Treaty was signed. One day after dropping off the General to an undisclosed designation, he got lost driving back. The more he drove, the more he realized he was in enemy territory. Eventually the only choice he had was to abroad a vehicle boat raft with his jeep; to go across the river. Once he boarded, he realized all the men on the boat raft was the enemy and they had weapons. The moment they were about to pull their weapons out on dad, someone jumped out of no where. The person that came out of no where, started to talk to the enemy with authority. They understood him and put their weapons back. Dad reached into his pockets and handed out Chocolate Bars to the enemy. They smiled and took the chocolate bars like they had been best friends. Dad was convenience that the person who jumped out in front of the enemy on the raft, wasn't on the raft when they left the shore line. There was no where to hide on the raft. The raft was all open. For a long time, he believed it was an angel that appeared out of no where. He was also thankful that he had the desire to trade his cigarettes rations for the other GI's Chocolate Bars. I asked dad a few times while writing this book and he would say that he couldn't remember. He remembers driving the General, getting lost and the raft but can't remember the details of each.

Son: How did you leave Korea after the war was over?

Dad: I think I went home. I was glad to get the Hell out of there. Go by army truck to get on ship.

Son: Do you remember the day you seen mom for the first time; holding her in your arms? Dads eyes watered up. Choked up. I've never seen dad choke up. A long minute passes.

Dad: I should remember but I don't.

Son: It's like dad wanted to say something but only he could cherish that moment, appreciate it because he was the one that personally experienced it. To anyone else, it would be just another after the war lover's reunion.

Son: If I remember right, mom lived with her parents and saved up her money while working full time, while dad was in the Korean War. Dad while in the Service lived on the bare essentials and sent the difference back to mom every month. Dad would do a lot of bartering. He would take the rations of cigarettes given to him by the service and trade them for Hershey bars. The two were saving up their money together to buy a piece of property to build their first home on.

Son: For me, events have always been easy to remember, but wasn't really big on remembering the specific dates to those specific events. But I got thinking at this point, especially with dad's larger than life real life story, I had to check. I kept putting it off and putting it off. And now I have no choice but to see what would come up on an internet search.

Son: It took me a day and a half to absorb the fact that Dad had his 21st birthday in the DMZ on the 38th parallel, the day before the North and South signed their peace treaty, 07-27-1953. Not only is this date after his 21st birthday, it is just shy of one day of being exactly four months after his wedding date of 03-28-1953. It's like historical mile stones to mark dad as the man to inspire boys to be men, men to be husband's that love their women unconditionally and husbands to be selfless fathers.

✠ Building Our Lives Together ✠

Son: The following notes from dad and I are random but all associated with the time of building and living in their first big square ranch home.

Son: Over a period of a few days of asking multiple questions to get dad to go into more details, he would always come back to this, "They wanted to know why I was building a big home. I just like to build. A three-bedroom home; must of knew, I liked to build. So, I built a three-bedroom home. I had no trouble selling them."

Son: I never saw dad and mom using and referencing to blue prints. Hardly, saw anyone; help dad and mom build their homes, except for the drivers for the lumber company, delivering the new house trusses, for each of the new homes. The driver would operate the crane attached to the flatbed to raise and lower the roof truss over and onto the house; while dad would position them and nail them down. They worked together like they were a construction crew, one truss at a time, until they were all in place to make the roof. He would place 2x4's perpendicular on the truss and nail them to the truss using number sixteen nails. Dad never used screws to build his homes. He used all nails; sixteen's or spikes, eights or penny's, and finish nails.

Son: Except for dad's first home, he built the trusses himself. It was a self-supporting roof, where the rafters were built in a way that they were putting the pressure on each other, at the peeks of each section of the roof versus using the interior walls of the house, for supporting the trusses. There is no attic space created with this style of truss. These rooms would be open from the floor to the roof.

Son: So, I went on to ask him other related questions to each of their homes that him and mom built together. Dad would do the basements, framing and all of the roughing in work; while mom focused on cleaning up after dad, cooking, painting, couple of kisses to motivate dad to dig trenches and the finishing work on their homes. Oh, plus watch my brother. After dad's first home, he would take me with him and I would play there on site; as I got older, I would help out more.

Son: Mom would tell me that her father didn't think Richard could build a home without prior experience, let alone a self-supporting roof without any fully built trusses. Despite her father's advice, she took dad to the hardware store and bought tools to build a home with. With a shovel, hammer and a hand saw they pursued building their lives together; one home at a time.

Son: Happiest Memory building your first home together with mom?

Dad: I built it like I knew how with a picture in my mind how it should go. Ranch home was a big home. Lots of room; did a lot of canning. Worked together, vacation together; week to two weeks vacation.

Son: Who taught you how to wire?

Dad: The same guy who taught my father-in-law.

Son: Mom would say a lot of women went to work in the factories while the men went to war. I vaguely remember, but I believe my mom did say she worked in the factory for a little while; like six months to a year or so, while dad was in the military. There was man in there that would hit on her but she kept telling him she was a married woman. I believe it was enough for her to quit the factory work and go to work for an insurance agency, for about six to seven years until I was born. Mom and dad waited seven years after they got married before having their first child.

Son: When dad got back from the service, he tried factory work. At the time there were a lot of factories in the Flint area. He said he could walk off the job at one factory and walk right into another factory and start working. There was a shortage of workers and factories had so much work to do, that they would hire anyone who came in off the street. He worked at the factory long enough, to be a union card carrying employee. Later when he retired in his sixties, he was able to use his union card to get body panel parts at discount, for restoring his 1984 Chevy Custom Truck.

Son: Dad didn't like working inside very long so he went to work for the local Power Company.

Dad: Power Company put gas line from Flint to Lake Huron. They didn't have automatic diggers; we had to dig everything by hand. When I got tired of shoveling, I went to reading meters. My feet got higher than my ass, I couldn't climb poles. I was afraid to loosen my hands around that pole. I had spurs; took awhile to climb a pole.

Son: When I was born, dad was twenty-eight years old, they had their first home already built.

Dad: My sweet heart was a hard worker and we took a lot of trips.

Son: Dad hunted with mom's dad. Hunted with brother-in-laws, car got stuck on off the road trail, on a hill. They all had to push except for the driver.

Son: Mom said she was hoping to get pregnant on your first trip out west together. She stopped all forms of contraception to make sure she did. Mom mentioned pulling off to the side of road to get view of the Grand Canyon. While making love, the police pulled up and knocked on window, telling the both of them to move on. (This might explain why I love to travel, view life in the big picture and get a tad jumpy around police coming. lol). Mom believed I was conceived on their first trip going out west.

Son: Even though I was under five years old and younger, I do remember some exciting and dramatic moments in the home with mom and dad.

Son: Dad bought a small dog that they named Patches because of the pattern of colors his fur was. The dog would bark off and on. Mom decided to let me feed the dog before Dad got home from work. I remember walking in the back yard. As a little guy it seemed big to me. I see patches happy and wagging his tail the closer I got to him. But for some reason when I gave him his dish of dog food, he bit me. I was shocked. Mom told me as I was going out the door to feed him, "watch out the dog might bite you." Patches did and my little fingers were hurting like no other. I ran back to the house to tell mom. Mom said she's telling dad and dad will get rid of the Patches. I said no; please don't tell dad. Can I try one more time first? She said she was still telling dad. And that's exactly what happened. Dad said the dog can't be trusted and he can't take a chance that Patches won't bit other children. I begged him and said please, one more time and then if Patches does then ok. That was my saddest moment in time. I didn't want Patches to leave because he bit me. So, I went outside and told Patches while he was wagging his tail, that he can't bit people anymore or he is going bye bye. I started to cry on the thought of losing Patches. Looking back at this made me realize, my love for animals, especially for dogs. So, the next day came and went like the day before. Despite all the long child like speeches I warned Patches about, he still bit me. This time, I tried to absorb the pain like a little boy man. I might of said a few cuss words as well. Mom notice I was holding and hiding my hand. She said, "Did Patches bite you?" I didn't say a word, knowing Patches would be taken away. As the tears were welling up in my eyes, I slowly nodded my head eyes. Tears' rolling down my cheeks, Mom says, "I'm telling your Dad." I felt helpless. Dad gave Patches away, quietly knowing he couldn't take a chance. The first day I walked out in the back yard, I was hoping to see Patches. Nope. Just pine trees, grass and an empty dog house. I stood there and cried.

Son: Not at the time, but looking back you knew the weekend was here because mom and dad loved to go out on every Friday or Saturday, every weekend religiously; year after year. Be it going dancing at the bars or playing cards. If it was playing cards, we went with them. If Christmas, must have been three years old. My cousins were watching me and we were decorating the tree.

Son: Mom was going into details on how our family was going to get bigger with having a new baby brother. Then one day mom walked in the door with a baby in her arms. It was my baby brother. I was so proud to be his brother. Mom said every time someone would come to their house, I would tell them I have a baby brother would you like to see him. Then I would walk them down the hallway to my brother's new room. I remember holding my brother in my arms. It was like holding mom and dad.

Son: Dad and mom would go on to building and remodeling homes together; while growing together as companions and best friends through out their lives and even through their senior years.

✝ Small Shed Cabin ✝

Son: Didn't know much on this, other than this cabin was the front lot apart of 4 to 10 total lots. Dad bought this group of lots to extend the end of the grassy dirt road drive with more cabins. He doesn't remember the timing, but it was before the A-frame on a lake in Gladwin County. Dad built the A-frame when my brother was less than a yr old and completely built before he was two yrs old, 1964 to 1965.

Son: This Small Shed Cabin was more like an over sized ice shanty with room for a small size twin size bunk beds to fit in and a small table to eat at. No bathroom, we had to use the outhouse. Don't remember having a refrigerator. There was just enough standing room for all four of us when the door was shut. Our room was basically sitting on the bunk bed. Us boys slept on the top bunk and mom and dad slept on the bottom bunk. It was like a family size tent but built like a cabin. It was an inexpensive place for mom and dad to stay at while being up North on the river with her mom and dad without staying at her mom and dad's place.

Son: I remember walking to my Grandma's for those awesome cookies she had and those countless games of marbles we played. Those awesome cookies were like a coconut chocolate gooey chew. I want to say the name of the cookie was Coconut Chews? I had to at least eat two of them before getting the strength to resist the temptation in asking for another one. I would glimpse at the kitchen cupboard drawer she kept them in, hoping to God she had more. The marble game's game board operates like the modern day Sorry® game board but with a different hole pattern. More like the outside edge pattern of the Red Cross® symbol. We would play that for hours. I loved it so much, dad made one for us to play as a family out of the scrap wood he had from building his homes.

Son: One time we arrived at the cabin when it was real dark. Seeing grandma's cabin was comforting until dad turned down the grassy dirt road going to our cabin. It was as though dad was driving us into a darken abyss. No dad! This is the wrong road. Dad assured me our cabin was just up ahead right next to the woods. The car lights lit up the small cabin. Dad turned off the car and said it was going to get real dark. That he would hold me in his arms until we got into the cabin. Mom tried unlocking the door with a flash light. It wasn't fast enough for me but I felt safe in dad's arms. The door opens and dad is lifting me up onto the top bunk. I must have passed out as soon as mom tucked me into bed, because I don't remember anything after that.

Son: During the day mom would walk us down the road that I got lost on and show us where the black berries that grew wild along the road. Turn around and walk to grandmas stay a tad then finish the walking trip to the CANDY STORE. It was a grocery store in the woods for the river side community, so they wouldn't have to make a long trip into town. All I could think about was the candy section in the grocery store, so I called it the CANDY STORE.

✝ Rental Home ✝

S on: Dad doesn't remember much about the Rental Home other than we stayed there until he finished building the colonial home.

Son: Mom was getting the Rental Home ready to live in while dad was building the Colonial style home. Painting walls, cleaning cupboards and floors.

Son: Dad and mom own the large ranch home, the lot and the colonial home building on the lot plus paying rent for the rental home; all at the same time. I believe I was close to four years old at this time. Dad and mom must have sold the large ranch home that late summer because it seemed like we move into the rental home that fall. Spent a winter there and moved into the Colonial the following summer.

Son: Our older cousins, on my mom's side, were watching me and my brother a lot while dad and mom worked on the colonial; every minute they could get.

Son: During the winter the back-storm door was flapping in the wind. I asked mom where that noise was coming from. She said it was the back-storm door and showed me. She said she will tell dad when he gets home and he'll fix it. She did and he did it just like that. It was always fascinating to watch dad build and fix things so easily. Dad had no former schooling with skilled trades, they came to him naturally. He said he could see it clearly in his mind and copied what he saw.

Son: Dad would love giving people tours of his new homes after he got them roughed in, roof on to keep the insides dry and warm from the colder rainy days. It felt like it was late fall, mom and dad would like to get us boys in bed by eight pm every night. Guessing Dad took me and his brother-in-law to see the progress of the colonial; just after sunset to maybe seven pm. It was defiantly real dark. Dad took us through the garage to the kitchen and basement entrance door. We were feeling our way around. Dad told me to stay close to him and hold his hand. Dad and his brother-in-law were trying to locate the light switch. For some reason they were having a tough time finding it. It didn't make since. I let go of dad's hand to help find the light switch. I don't remember anything after that. Thinking I blacked out tumbling down the stairway and onto the cement basement floor. My head throbbing with pain … a lot. I heard my dad's voice as I was coming to. Son you fell down the stair steps. You have a big bump on your head. I'm taking you to the hospital. It felt like a long wait in the old school emergency room but my dad was with me.

Son: Next thing I know, I was coming through the Rental Home's front door and mom greeted us. Dad laid me on the floor. I laid there while mom asked dad a million questions. We didn't have smart phones back then. We had to go to the nearest pay phone and hope to God the person we were calling would answer the phone. We didn't have answering machines back then either. Dad and mom were really calm, acted like it wasn't a big thing but kept checking up on me.

✝ Colonial ✝

Son: I want to say in the fall of 1963. I remember walking in the tall grass, viewing it with my three-year-old eyes with mom and dad. They were talking about how they bought this lot to build a new home on it and where the rooms would be.

Son: Shortly afterwards dad was burning the tall grass that he had heaped up in rows. I was watching dad manage the burning rows beside mom, in the back yard of the large square ranch home. I wanted to go be with dad. She walked me to dad and she told me to be very careful. When I got to dad, he said we should go back because he was going to add gas and torch the whole lot.

Son: On the nice weather days, dad would take me to the Colonial home as he was roughing it in. There was no roof on the home yet. Dad was up on a ladder and cutting 2x4's with a skill saw. 2x4 in one hand and the skill saw in another. Now day's people would say that was like super unsafe. This was back in the day when people had common sense and safety was just common sense. If it made common sense then it was safe. If it's not common sense then it was unsafe. Dad was zipping along and making good progress like he naturally does everyday. But this time the skill saw was still running when he rested it on his knee. My eyes got big. The skill saw ripped through his jeans right into his skin. Blood came gushing out. Dad remained calm, like he knew what he was doing. He put the skill saw down and applied pressure to his wound to stop it from bleeding. He told me to run home and tell mom that we needed to go to the hospital as soon as possible. We were still living in the big ranch home at the time. My messenger boy mentality kicked my short four-year-old legs into high gear and was home in no time. I must of have been girbbling. Yup, that's a new word I just added to my dictionary of make-believe words. My mom was saying stuff like. Slow down son. You're not making sense. So, I decided to just keep repeating myself until mom started moving in dad's direction.

Son: Mom says something like, Richard. Omg! In no time we were in the emergency room, dad was stitched up and back building on the house all in the same day. Yes. This is not a typo. Mom wanted dad to rest and heal up. But all dad had on his mind was getting back to building. Dad said it came natural to him and he loved building. This was more proof he did.

Son: Dad must have had different types of fear of height when climbing the twelve story rope ladders and telephone poles versus walking on a four inch wide top plate holding the second floor walls together. All while the delivering lumber yard driver was lifting the truss off the flatbed with a hydraulic lift, onto the second-floor walls to become a new roof. My dad walked on those four-inch-wide top plates like he was a professional wire walker. I was amazed at how dad was nailing the truss in place with spikes with no safety harness on. No fear. Within an hour or two, both of them had hung and secured those entire trusses together; that now made the roof on dad's new two-story home.

Son: The day we moved in the Colonial, mom was all happy and excited to be in a bigger home.

Son: I never questioned how dad could do everything; forty-hour job, build homes then still have time to make eye contact while playing with us at our individual levels, as a family. He was never in a rush, but yet he stayed consistently busy. I couldn't detect any pain, frustration and or despair in the tone of his voice, in the touch of his hands or in his eyes. Dad always made time to hang out with us every night, even if it was for a few minutes. It was the best minutes of my day and my relationship with my dad. He would always take mom out on the town on the weekends; either Friday or Saturday nights; every week, every year. Mom would harmonize it so that we looked forward to it as well. She was a late nighter who loved to sleep in every morning. One of our cousins would come over to babysit us until mom and dad got back late; midnight, sometimes 2 AM in the morning.

Son: They had two vehicles; a car and a truck. If dad had to sell the truck, he would hitch a ride to work with a work friend, so that mom would have the car incase something came up.

Son: Dad always made us feel like we had plenty of food even though we didn't. Looking back, dad and mom were putting as much money as they could into land and homes. Dad showed it best when it came to ice-cream. He would ask me if I wanted some ice-cream. I would say yes, two scoops please. He would deliver the two scoops as requested in my empty bowl, started to walk away, turned back and put another scoop in my bowl. I would say, hey. I don't want it. He would say; you can never have enough ice-cream. Then laugh.

Son: We didn't get settled in for too long; dad and mom started to talk about building another home. Dad bought the lot, had the basement put in and capped off with the sub floor before winter hit.

Son: We lived n the Colonial for about two years.

Son: One of those Falls or Winters, Dad taught kids from a local youth development club on how to wire a light in 2 weeks. It was a class of about twelve to fifteen boys. He had made make shift mini angle top desk to hold their projects on; while standing next to it. They built it on the basement floor then wired it on their angle top desks. Dad let me help him be the errand boy. Dad loved teaching people skills they could use for the rest of their lives. Dad smiled a lot and made their experience a personal self accomplishment. One week he had them build their three foot by sixteen-inch 2x4 sample wall size with some thin plywood to hold it together. The next week they put the lighting fixture on and wired to it. Once they were done, he would go around and put the power and ground wires on the battery terminals; to see if they had wired it up correctly. If they did, the light would turn on. If not, they would have to rewire it and try again. By the time class was done they all knew how to wire a light.

Son: The following spring the concrete floor in the garaged caved in. The cement caved in a pattern was like there was mini sink holes clustered together. We would play on them like we were pirates looking for buried treasure. Dad busted up the three foot by four-foot chunks in the garage into smaller sizes, loaded them up into a wheel barrel and used them to build a six to eight-foot-wide arched side walk from the front porch to the driveway. He fitted the pieces together like they were a paver puzzle, with space in between each piece. Once done, he had new sand dumped into the garage to build it back up to level. Rented his own motorized mini cement mixer, had a brother-in-law/friend help him make cement and re-poured the garage floor by hand. It was perfect.

✝ A-Frame Cabin ✝

Son: My brother was born in April 1963. Dad and mom would love drive along the River that ran from her mom and dad's cabin to the Dam in Gladwin County. Dad and mom had their shed type cabin just down the road from her mom and dad's cabin. On their way up to and on their back home, they would drive along the river looking for a lot to buy on wider part of the river. The wider part of the river was created by the power generating dam on the river. About midway on the east side of the river was an inlet lot; stumpy looking and a third of lot was under water compared to its neighboring lots. By appearance it was undesirable inlet lot, with an awesome beach. It had a for sale sign nailed to one of the stumps with a number to call. I can imagine mom and dad parking their car by the side of the road, walking into the lot and seeing the beach for the first time. Looking into each other eyes their faces lite up as they took off their shoes to walk on the sandy beach. They reach out for each other's hand and walk the sandy beach waters together. As they walk back to the car dad takes the sign off the stump so no one else will buy the lot from underneath them. They lived in the town where they meet each other at the free movies and the lot was owned by someone who lived in the town just southwest from there. The summer of 1963, my mother registers the deed to that inlet lot in both of their names.

Son: Dad worked for a Utility Company that was replacing all of their cedar power line poles with bigger pretreated poles. Power lines were either going up higher or either under ground. Dad asked for a pile of those cedar poles and they gave them to him ALL for FREE. Guessing the spring or summer of 1964, he got one or two trailers fully loaded. Dad took me with him to his brother's saw mill. Dad told me not to move and just watch. They loaded each pole into a cradle and cut them into perfect 4.0 in x 6.0 in support beams. They didn't get very far It was insanely noisy, dark and I wanted to go home. Dad took me home and went back to finish the job; along with cutting the cedar telephone poles into 1.0 in x 6.0 in slabs for roof boards.

Son: During the summer of 1964, dad had assembled the 4x6 cedar beams in the letter A pattern. He mitered the top A part of beams so that their tips were flush with one another. Then about two feet down from the tip of the A, he put a cross member to hold the tip of the A stronger. Then down about 10 feet from the tip he put another cross member to form the letter A. This added strength plus this was the base of the second floor. Then one more time, about one to two feet off the ground for the first floor. He laid cement block around the foundation; two to three blocks high. He assembles this all by himself; using a long big drill bit to bore holes for the long thick bolts to hold each part of each A pattern structure together. Once assembled, he asked his brother-in-laws on mom side and their families to help pull each of the A's up in the air. Using a big thick long tow rope, anyone who wanted to pull each A up, got at the end of the rope and pulled it up with all of their might. Priceless. One by one they were all lifted into place and Dad secured them together using the 1.0 in x 6 .0 in slabs of cedar. It was beautiful sight.

Son: Dad had tons of sand dumped in front yard to the lake; to even it up with the neighboring lots. Over the next few years when it rained harder than normal and the dam didn't release the water at the same ratio; the water eroded a lot of the sand out into the lake. It made the beach even better. One-year dad and mom lost a third of their front lawn; that year dad and mom piled us in the family station wagon to go get a pile of large rocks. The rocks were so heavy that the station wagon's tail end was almost scrapping the road and the tires were squashed out so bad that it looked like they were ready to pop. No matter how much we tried to convince dad it was unsafe, he said it was ok, we'll go slowly. He didn't want to come back for more unless he had a truck. The rock wall seemed to work out and more sand was hauled in.

Son: Growing up with dad and mom at the A-Frame Cabin with that awesome beach on wider part of the river; would become some of the best memories our family had together. Some summer's mom and us boys stayed up north for weeks at a time, while dad stayed home and went to work Monday thru Friday. He would come up to the cabin on Fridays after work then leave to go straight to work early Monday mornings.

Son: During one of the summers in the early 1970's. We were living on the 80 Acre Farm. Mom and us boys were staying up at the Cabin while Dad stayed at home to go to work. My brother and I were playing around the A-Frame Cabin yard; like we do every other Sunny Summer Weekday. Mom signaled us to come in the cabin. Mom explained that Dad was in a bad accident and in the hospital. I couldn't believe it. What? Looking at mom repeating herself, with the helpless tone she used, I asked what we can do. She said we need to leave in a half hour. She was shutting down the inside of the Cabin and she asked us boys to do the outside. I put the canvas on the boat, made sure it was secured to the dock and tree on shore line, mowed as much of the lawn as I could. When mom was coming out the Cabin door, she asked if we needed to use the bathroom, put the lawn mower up and get in the car ASAP. Mom didn't cry in front of us if she was, she had the look on her face, she wanted to be by dad's side but couldn't. When we got home, we stayed home and mom went right to the hospital to see dad.

It was several hours, before mom returned with the news; that dad was lucky to be alive. Dad's chest ribs were busted up by the steering wheel caused by the impact of a direct head on collision. It was a foggy morning. Dad tried to avoid the on coming truck. But every time dad moved away from the on coming vehicle, it followed him. His chest slammed into the steering wheel and the glass shattered all over his body and onto his face. It took awhile from the EMS to clean the shattered glass off his face, and then moved him out of his truck. It took him six weeks to heal up. Mom was very supportive and after being a few days home dad was back to his witty old self. This was back when wearing a seat beat was an option and windshields weren't shattered proof.

Son: Minus the heart stopping moment we had with dad's accident; being at the Lake was like being in heaven; well maybe a taste of. We played in the sand with our toys, building sand castles, blowing them up with fire-crackers, tubing, water skiing, hide-n-seek, telling stories and playing chubby bunny around the camp fire, going for monster ice-cream cones, fishing, canoeing, driving on the back roads looking for deer, going to play with our cousins on mom's side farther north up the river. Mom's other sister's all bought lots and built cabins by her mom and dad's cabin. Fire works on Fourth of July. What was even cooler was mom's mother's birthday was on the fourth of July. She was born 07-04-1901. It was easy to remember how old she was based on the year. If it was 1980, she was 79 years old. When we got more adventurous, we went over and around the south side of the dam, to canoe farther down the river. It was like Louis and Clark to us; wanting to see what was around the next bend in the river. Hydro boarding. The most coolest ever was swinging on a barn rope hanging from a pine tree, that was leaning over the water. We would pull the rope back to the shore line and hop on the big knot at the end of the rope. We would swing like thirty feet out into the water and then air drop into the water. It was more awesome then diving off a diving board. Aaah the memories and these are all the general bullet points. Each one of these is a chapter by themselves. Those memories are priceless.

Son: We had an outhouse for a few years until dad plumped the cabin. It was like AWESOME. No more taking a flashlight out in the middle of dark night just to go to pee. The scariest moments were when we got inside the out house by ourselves. The darkness and the noises would scare the pee and poop right out of us. Our wipe and go speeds broke Genius Book records. After a few scary times we always made sure we went to pee before going to bed.

Son: Dad and mom loved family and loved to entertain. A few weekends out of the Summer the Cabin, the front and back yards were filled with people, campers and tents. It would feel and look like a camp ground site, piled onto one small lot. The poor toilet was being flushed so much, it didn't know if it was coming or going. It would back up, so we had to flush it the old school way. If peeing, don't flush the toilet; if pooping, please for God's sake flush the toilet. These two rules seemed to fix the problem, unless it was raining :(

Son: If waking up to the smells of eggs and sausage breakfast on Saturday mornings didn't work; dad would wake us up to the sounds of power tools. Once we got up he would say, "What do you think this is a rest camp?" Laugh. Then cook us breakfast.

Son: Ok, for those of you who are still curious about what Chubby Bunny is? And what is Chubby Bunny doing around a campfire? We did this when we had a nice size group staying with us at the Cabin and or our cousins came over to play on dad's beach. We would start our campfires just as the sun was about to go down for the day; awesome view in itself. Yup. And being on the east side of the river we would see some gorgeous sunsets. Ok Chubby Bunny.

Since this can be a competitive campfire pass time, we made sure we had three to four bags of marshmallows on stand by. We would decide which direction around the campfire we would go, and then the first person would put a marshmallow into their mouth without eating it and say the words "Chubby Bunny." The group would smile and be thinking with their faces; this is going to be hilarious. This game defiantly identifies who has the biggest mouth. Lol. Ok, so most everyone gets by round one, unless you're like two or three years old. Lol. Round two, shove another marshmallow into your mouth without eating it as well, then say, "Chubby Bunny." Yup, you guest it. People started gagging while most every one was laughing at them. A few would start to have doubts when they heard the gagging and started to up chuck themselves. One by one, the smaller mouth competition gagged out. Some vomited their slimy pile of marshmallows onto the campfire. The slimy goop would become black chard ashes floating in the air. The higher the number of marshmallows a person had to stuff into their mouths without eating them; the harder it was to say "Chubby Bunny." A person had to say it clear enough for everyone else around the campfire could hear the words, "Chubby Bunny." If they couldn't, they defaulted to losing by poor communication. This was a total blast until the same person kept winning all the time. Hmm… I'll give you one guess who that person was. Dang; how did you know it was me? Sixteen marshmallows all in my big mouth and I said "Chubby Bunny" with the satisfaction of beating everyone around the campfire, every time. It was priceless seeing the expressions on everyone's faces. And to play it up, I acted as though I was gagging before I said, "Chubby Bunny." Some would start to gag themselves, die laughing and staring in amazement that someone could actually hold sixteen marshmallows in their mouth. As a repeated grand champion, I would finish my routine with graciously letting my mouth pile of marshmallows drip and ooze out of my mouth onto the campfire. Yeeeeees! Chubby Bunny anyone?

Son: These stories are just the tip of the ice-berg of countless memories we made as a family. These good times were all created from that one-day dad and mom saw past the stumpy wooded inlet lot; stopped, walked in the sandy watery beach and then took the for sale sign off one of those stumps as they walked back to their car.

☦ Small Ranch ☦

S on: Dad and mom were hoping to build this small ranch and sell it at a profit; to help pay off the Colonial Home. The Colonial was mom's favorite home of all of the homes they built. Dad and mom ended up getting into a financial squeeze. They were only getting buyers for the Colonial. They had no choice but to sell the Colonial.

Son: I was six or seven years old when dad built this home.

Son: I was playing in the yard of the New Small Ranch home one day when I saw dad slipped off the roof and fell on the ground. I was shocked, but not old enough to know the impact of falling off the roof of a single-story home was. Dad was almost done finishing the roof. All he had to do was to put the cap on the peak.

Dad: Son run home and tell mom; I fell off the roof. I'm ok.

Son: I put on my messenger mind hat and got my legs moving in high gear. I wasn't a real fast runner. I was more worried about forgetting what I was supposed to tell her. Dad was counting on me and I didn't want to waste time forgetting.

Son: All I could think about was the time mom asked me to go tell dad supper was on the table and ready. I got half way from the Colonial to the Small Ranch and I forget what mom said. So, I had to walk all the way back home to the Colonial and ask mom what I was to tell dad. She said supper is ready. I got walking and forgot again. I was embarrassed. No matter how hard I tried to remember I forgot. I walked back and asked mom a second time. She said think of food. That worked. I made it the third time and told dad supper is ready. We hopped in the car and went home to some good cooking dinner.

Son: I made it back to the Colonial and I remembered, Mom dad fell off the roof and he's ok. Mom said what? How can dad fall off a roof and be ok? You sure you got the message, right? I said yes. I saw dad fall off the roof and he get back up. Mom said are you lying? This doesn't make sense at all. If you're lying and I get down there and find out your dad didn't fall off the roof, I'm going to wash your mouth out with soap. Thinking to myself that's true; mom always does what she says. I said it's the truth. Mom was convinced I was a liar until we arrived to the New Small Ranch home. Dad was walking on the roof. Mom says, look there's nothing wrong with your dad. I know, I said. She looked back at dad and said; Richard, did you fall off the roof? Dad said yes and when I hit the ground I bounced right back up on the roof. He laughed. Mom said this is serious; we should go to emergency room right now to get x-rays; to see if you're ok. Dad said why don't you and my son come up here and help me finish this cap before night falls. Mom followed close up behind me to make sure I didn't fall off the latter. Transition from latter to roof was scary as all hell. Once on the roof, I crawled slowly to the top of the roof with mom on my side. I straddle the peak of the roof with my little legs where dad was putting the cap on. Mom went back down and got some shingles to be cut into more cap pieces. When dad had enough, she stopped carry up shingles and started cutting the cap pieces. When she cut one, she would hand it to me and then I would hand it to dad. I just had witnessed Dad in his peaceful smooth ways get mom up on the roof; he finished the cap that night with his family versus going to the emergency room.

Son: Dad and mom made us feel like a family no matter what we did. They were never in a hurry, but kept consistently busy.

Son: Mom's sisters and their families showed up to the Colonial for mom's birthday on April 4th of 1966 or 67. Mom loved to be the center of attention and she was getting it like on overload; especially in the home she loved the most. But dad had a surprise. Her sisters and their families didn't just show up for a birthday party. They showed up to help move them out of their Colonial into the Small Ranch that evening. Oh mom was pissed. She thought it was a joke at first but when everybody started loading up their trucks with furniture and everything else that could fit in they did. She got so mad she sat in the padded cloth rocking chair. She would say, "I'm not moving today. I want my birthday in the Colonial not the Ranch!" Everyone ignored her.

Son: When everything was moved but mom sitting in the rocking chair. One of the brother-in-laws asked, now what do we do? Dad told them to pick her up and put her in the back of the truck. They laughed. Mom cried. They carried her in the rocking chair, to the back of the truck and slide her to back side of cab wall window. She was begging dad, not to do it. He said, let's let the first day of staying in the new house, be on your birthday. Wouldn't you want to wake up the next day after your birthday in our new home? Once they got to the Small Ranch, they lifted her out of the truck and carried her into the house, chair and all. When they got to the new smaller kitchen; all of her sister's and their families were in there packed, for the number two surprise birthday party. Mom is still mad and wants to go back to the Colonial. Everyone breaks out with," Happy Birthday to you. Happy Birthday to you…" song and mom melted, smiled and said thank you for all the help in moving. Everything was going to be ok.

Son: This would be mom's toughest move in moving to a new place to live with dad for the rest of their lives together. This move she didn't want to move. All the other moves she was looking forward to a new place to live, along with all the new routines it generated. It was awesome that Dad was sensitive enough to know this and tried to comfort mom as much as he could; by including this move with all her loved ones. Then gentle enough to make it a birthday surprise, at the beginning of the move and then again at the end of the move. Brilliant; from presentation to delivery, in accepting this is where fate wanted them to be and move on.

Son: That following Christmas dad and mom took us all to Florida to spend two weeks with grandma. Dad and mom were all naturals at: taking turns driving, supportive of each other and with us boys while on the beach, playing shuffle board and giving us playing marbles with grandma time. Looking back, I think dad intentionally insisted on going to Florida that year, to ease mom's pain in having to give up the big Colonial home, to live in the small Ranch home. It worked perfect; mom loved her Florida and being with her mother.

Son: The big surprise came when heading back from Florida. After asking mom and dad, when are we going to be home for the nth time; Mom gave us a different answer while sitting down for breakfast at a restaurant. Dad had gotten up and went to the bathroom when mom busted out with, boys we are taking a detour that will add another day to our trip back home. She said it in the tone of sober excitement with a tinge of reservation. We wanted to tell you earlier, but didn't so that you could focus on enjoying being in Florida versus wanting to leave earlier. The suspense was pushing me to the edge of my restaurant chair. Mom must have seen it in our eyes so she stopped with the intro and went to, we bought a dog and we're going to go pick him up today. I like lost it. No way. This trip went from way cool to absolutely awesome. Dad came back from the bathroom and added to the conversation with, I called them and they know we're on there way. Looking back, I didn't think, how did they find out about this dog in Ohio, when we live in Mid-Michigan? No internet search engines. Some how they found this family that raised English Springer Spaniels that loved little children; and in this case; racing dogs. Yeah. Are we getting in the racing dog business?

Son: As we were sitting in the kitchen living room of this breeder's home, she brought out two dogs one at a time. The first was happy and beautiful; yup this is the one, I'm thinking. Then the second, she said the reason she left him for last is because, he's a racer and he's won ribbons and one is a first-place ribbon. She races him regularly and was hoping if we took him, that we would continue to race him. She explained how she deliberately gets in the dog's face while they are eating so that they'll relax and learn to be comfortable with it. This training will make them be good around little children and other animals. After petting the first dog for a few minutes, she brought out Smudge. Smudge got his nick name for the white brown speckled patch around his nose area. Beautiful, friendly and instant bonding; Smudge has my vote. Tough decision for the rest of the family for various reasons; she should keep her race dog, etc. So, we did a once more introduction with the dogs. This first was so cud able. Then Smudge the instant bonder. Yup he's got my vote again. After discussing, would it be ok to have Smudge even though he is a racer; that will more than likely not be raced again in his life. She said she would greatly miss Smudge but must depart with the dogs and it might as well be with someone who wants him, even if they don't want to race him.

Son: Getting back on the road to home with Smudge lying in our laps made the hours feel like minutes.

Son: I can't remember if it was the first Summer or second and last Summer we were in the Small Ranch; this scary torrential rainy tornado hit our neighbor. I was ok up until the fire truck came through our subdivision telling us personally with their amplified speaker. "Go to the southwest corner of your basement immediately. A tornado has touched down and it is coming this way." They were driving slowly and they circled the subdivision twice. As this was occurring, it was raining heavy and harder than I could remember. Mom and dad took us to the basement immediately. Dad took the living room couch down the basement and flipped it over so that our bodies were lying down on the back-rest pad of the couch. He butted the two couch top edges together, for all four us to lie on; so that the back of the couches was lying flat on top of the basement cement floor. Then dad put the cushions on top of us to protect us from possible debris. The power went out, it was now pitch dark in our new basement and now we couldn't see anything. Dad went to look for a flash light and a battery-operated radio. I was saying, NO. Don't go Dad! Stay here with us. He went anyways and mom comforted us. They worked together like pros.

Son: After dad showed up with the flash light, I must have knocked out big time. Don't remember nothing; but being waked up out of the blue. Mom saying, wake up. Dad is coming back to carry you up stairs. The basement is flooded and the couch is soaked. And if the power comes back on, we could all get electrocuted. A couple minutes later dad is reaching out to me to pick me up, while he walks in the water. It looked like he was walking in about six to eight inches of water. The rain had stopped and we were all back into our beds.

Son: Looking back I think that tornado storm that flooded the Small Ranch's basement, was the motivator for dad and mom to start looking for a bigger safer home to live in again.

Son: Dad and mom started talking about where they can build their next home. The current subdivision they were living in had no more available corner lots. Dad just didn't want to build a home; he wanted it to have a good view and located in the best section of the neighborhood.

Son: The church mom liked to go to was in the process of locating itself from one town to the next. I want to say the people were friendlier at the new town. One Sunday going to the church in the new town, dad noticed a farm up for sale.

Son: Mom like the idea of moving so much she started packing, items we weren't using. They found a farm about 2 miles west of the Small Ranch home, that they were ooing and gooing about, every time we went and came back from church. After thinking about it throughout the week dad and mom decided to stop in after Church the next Sunday to make an offer to purchase it. I was ecstatic thinking about all the things we could do on the farm. Dad was talking about getting cats, horses, roosters, hens, farming equipment, etc.

Son: An added kicker to this experience was when I was reading in moms memoirs, before writing this book, she talked about how she would spend hours sitting up in a tree, on her suburb city back yard looking at the farm land; watching and listening to the animals come and go on it.

Son: This was who mom and dad were together. Curious as a couple in going to new places, building and buying homes to flip while making good memories in each one of them; to the point of forgetting about everything when on the beach, enjoying their cabin to the max like clock work. The alarm goes off; they switch to doing something new and fun.

Son: Building their lives together was defiantly about to kick into high gear.

✝ Eighty Acre Farm ✝

Son: That following Sunday we did stop. The house was older than old school. The big yard was full of huge trees with three different size barns out back and possibly those woods in the distance. Just before we stop though, dad decided to drive down the road on the west property line, to see how far back the farm runs back from the main road. It was quite lengthy from an 8 to 9-year old's perspective. By the looks on Dad's face, he was intently studying the view of an eighty-acre farm on its side. At the rate dad was building homes and cabins, he was probably thinking of a zillion and one things he could do with it. Dad stops the car, and says; see that fence row, that's the property line. The woods are included in the farm. Then does a farmer's u turn on the gravel road, by rolling a couple of feet into the ditch line. We're freakn as he's doing the choppy u turn dance in the middle of the road. He did it. If I just closed my eyes, my body would have felt like he knew exactly what he was doing.

Son: Driving down the driveway to the farm house was like epic new options dancing in my mind on how to grow up moment. My eyes queued in on a swing hanging from the huge swamp oak tree branch; like two stories up. I asked if I could swing on it and boy did I. I heard there was a God who listens to our prayers so I started praying up a storm of, oh God please LET mom and dad get this farm.

Son: In a couple of blinks, we all piled in the car and we were leaving heaven. Dad and mom were excited and talking like there's a really good chance that they were going to get the farm.

Son: When dad and mom starting sharing the decision with moms' side of the family; they were telling dad and mom, that they were crazy for spending $40,000.00 for an 80-acre farm in 1967 -68. Dad ignored them and said they didn't know what their talking about.

Son: Don't remember how they found out, but they got the farm. It was Christmas all year long big time! Mom was going to be able to leave the home she dreaded to move in.

Son: Ok. This was a good back drop for starting this chapter but we need to hear from dad, what he remembers while being on the farm, before going into more details of my experiences with dad and mom interacting with each other.

Dad: Working for a Power Company two towns over, I got a chance to go to Power Dam to see my mother's side of the family a lot. Ma had sister out there, nine or eleven children. It might have been twenty years, since I've last seen them. Worked there for awhile then transferred back to Flint.

Dad: I worked; still time off to take vacation, up north played as a family, played together.

Dad: My wife cried a lot at the farm. Didn't pay attention to it. She would say something. I would say something. I wouldn't drag it out; too much to do.

Son: You think maybe the high sugar she was having, before she knew it, caused her depression; her crying more?

Dad: Founding out she had diabetes saved her life. Cut the sugar right out. I showed no sympathy for sugar.

Son: Didn't you both end up going to a Marriage Retreat?

Dad: Seems like a big group of us; Summer time. Go through discussions to bring up issues. Isolated from everything else, at some one else's place; so, had time to talk. We weren't going anywhere.

Son: I remember mom talking about it being a break through for her in communicating with you. Mom loved to talk and you loved to show your love by your actions. But I think the difference was like you mentioned you couldn't go anywhere or do anything. So, all you could do was have long talks with mom. It's like now with you. I haven't felt closer to you then in these last few months of writing your book with you; by asking you a million questions. All you have been is talking; you have a wealth of information, wisdom and compassion.

Son: Dad some how had connections. Got a good deal on a bar style pool table while on a route reading meters for the utility company. The whole family played tons of pool. Dad liked to play it more than mom, but when mom did, she gave dad a run for his money. When there was more than two of us wanting to play pool; dad would insist on playing 9 Ball, so we all could be playing together now versus taking turns with dad. It wasn't so much as the love of playing pool; it was the Art of Having Fun Together as a Family. The most memorable ones are playing with something that is inexpensive versus buying expensive toys and having expensive hobbies.

Son: Before the apple trees died off on the farm, after dad and mom bought it, the spy apple tree was producing spy apples the size of one and half softballs. They were like three to four apples put together. Dad would pick em and mom would cook em into a pie to die for. Mom would invite her sister's families to the farm on the holidays. They got to saying, only if you're cooking them awesome apple pies. As I got older, I would say mom you should be mass producing these. She would say; if I had to do it as work, I wouldn't enjoy making them.

Son: Dad and mom got the idea of and pursuing development of the whole 80 farm into a new subdivision, with the woods being a park, bike trail all the way around the outside, club house and roads named after our family first names. They had the blue print where everything would be at. It was so cool looking. They were going to air drop houses in with helicopters. The county planning commission was bought in. But as time went on nothing was happening. Dad and mom had to put like a chunk of money down to get this Company to set in motion the whole project. Blue Prints, etc. But nothing; mom was getting more pissed then a boiling pot of water and dad was quietly supporting her. I think they got a lawyer, sued this Company for scamming them out of their money. I want to say they didn't get their money back because the company justified it was the cost of their simple blueprint drawing of the project, they went bankrupt and left town. This didn't stop dad. While my mom was giving this Company Reps hell, dad was calm and must of have been thinking about Plan B in developing the farm.

Son: Looking back, it was like mom was getting adrenaline rushes from building homes together with dad. And this was their moment in kicking it into high gear the building of their lives together, with each other through this subdivision project.

Son: Once mom came to grips that they weren't going to get any reprieve with this company, she quickly fell in love with dad's Plan B version of subdividing the farm. Break the farm up into larger chunks; One twenty acre plot for $20,000; that later got split into two 10's, about four 2.5 acre plots for about $10,000, an 8.9 acre plot to built my first house on with dad, I think 2 or 3 five acre plots for 7 to $10,000 each. Most of these lots were access by the west property line road side. Inflation started to kick in. Mom's side of the family started to see dad and mom reap the benefits of higher real estate prices. The added surprise bonus was the Utility Company dad was working for, was thinking about putting up a huge metal tower power lines on dad's property, so they bought 10 acres for $17,000. The Utility Company didn't know if they were going to head west or south, so they bought land in both directions. Plus get this, dad and mom got the property rights to farm that land, tax and rent free. They got the best of both worlds. I believe dad and mom ended up with about twenty acres to themselves. Minimum estimated total earnings of Plan B $61,000. Plus, the money from selling their twenty acres in the late 80's to early 90's.

Son: Playing cards around the table. Every weekend mom and dad would take turns going to each of mom's sister's home; to play cards with their husbands and wives. Mom had three sisters, so there was eight of them around the table playing pinnacle, rummy, up the river down the river, and any game they could play boys against the girls with. My dad and mom's older sister were the comedians in the group. If dad wasn't saying something witty, mom's older sister was. Everyone was always laughing. However, sometimes the sisters would start yelling at each other; mom jumps in with no fear. The card game comes to a grinding halt. The brother-in-laws are all quietly watching these sisters go at it. They would be like a couple of inches face to face. Then at the right moment dad would say something witty pertaining to what they were fighting about. The sisters would stop yelling. Look at dad and started laughing. Her older sister would pipe in and all of them are now laughing and acting like the fight never happened. Brilliant mental therapy for the sisters; I can see now why they all loved to get together one night on the weekend, every week for years.

Son: Instead of dad building a new home most every day of the week after coming home from work, it was now remodeling the whole farm house. First, he ripped out all the extra doors in the house. Why so many doors? Back then, during the winter months they would only heat key rooms; every where you turned was a door. Then dad and mom would go room by room; dad would do all the dirty work of ripping out the horse haired plaster covering little strips of wood tacked to the 2x4's. Yes, these were the real 2x4's before they went to 1.5 x 3.5 two by fours. So, dad would have to build out the new to the old. For about 2 to 3 days we would see the horse hair plaster dust on everything. This was considered their drywall back in the day. Dad replaced with the new sheets of gypsum board drywall. After dad mudded it, mom would wall paper it. Wall paper was the latest in decorating the interior walls of homes.

Son: We got a few years of storage out of the old big barn that used to be the home of the original horse farm. Over the decades of strong storms against her, the barn started to have a dangerous lean to it. Dad told us we couldn't play in it any more, in fear it might fall on us. He eventually tore down the barn with the intent of using the outside barn boards as their kitchen wall paneling. Every day after school me and mom were out next to the barn pulling nails out of the barn siding boards, so that dad could cut them to size when he got home from work.

Son: After being on the 80 acre farm for a few years, mom started threatening dad divorce; crying in bed a lot and being depressed. The first few times mom actually walked out the door on dad and either drive the car away or start walking down the road. I got caught up in it and begged dad to say something, go get mom dad we need her. He wouldn't budge. He wouldn't say a thing. He had a peaceful look on his face. There was no anger emitting from his body. I didn't understand it. So, I asked dad, why aren't you going after mom? And dad said with an assured voice tone, she'll be back. I would say; how do you know? And he would reply, because no one else can put up with her. Then he would peacefully laugh. Dad would go on with his day like nothing ever happened. A few hours later mom would show up and act like nothing ever happened. The both would be kissing each other before bed time.

Son: When I got home from school mom would talk my ear off about how she wished dad would like to go to church and be more of a Christian man. That's when mom and I started to read the Bible a lot independently and talk about it before dad came home. She would be talking about being unequally yoked together. I was hoping our conversations would extinguish her thoughts of divorcing dad but would end up crying myself to sleep a lot of nights, praying to this God that would keep mom and dad together. I couldn't stand the thought of dad and mom being divorced. Dad would eventually go more regularly with mom to church. I started to feel like I was a mediator between mom and dad. I would ask dad why he didn't want to go to church with us. Dad would say, he has things to do verses sitting around and talking. I would say there is always something to do. He would say, church is for women and children to give them something to believe in. I believe there's a God. Look at all the details in the world. The ocean stops at the shoreline so we have land to live on. The air we breathe. With what time I have I need to keep moving. Looking back in my life while raising my three children by myself, I couldn't agree more with dad. Time can be short and we need to spend it on the people and things that matter the most in our lives versus socializing with people.

Son: Dad later professed Christ as his personal Lord and Savior. This comforted mom more than anything else in their marriage. Even though dad wasn't involved in the church as much as mom was, mom was comforted by the fact; that dad was going to be in heaven with her, to continue their life after this life on earth.

Son: Animals galore. One by one, dad would let us add to our family of farm animals. The icon of the whole group was Smudge. Smudge would go around checking up on all his animal friends. Smudge would even let the kittens nurse on him when their mothers were not around. His tities got so red and sore but he acted like it didn't hurt him. The two horses, his dog friend Toby, up to thirty cats at one time – yes thirty, two roasters, three hens and three rabbits. Mom would make it clear that if we boys didn't take care of all these animals, that she was going to have dad get rid of them. I confirmed with dad. Dad said yes. He got the animals for us to learn responsibility. If we didn't want that responsibility then he would find homes for them; with people who would love them and take care of them. I looked forward every day hanging out with all the animals, every day after school. Going from one animal to the other to make sure they were all feed and had something to drink. They became my friends. I got so emotionally attached with them, that every time one of them would pass away, I would cry for days. I would tell mom, that one of the animals passed on. She would say, she'd tell dad and he'll take care of it. Most of the time, I would be there right next to dad, while he was burying the animal. He would ask me where should we bury so and so? I would offer a suggestion. He would agree, get the shovel and ask me if I wanted to dig the hole. I couldn't at first because I would be so emotionally attached to the animal. I would watch dad peacefully dig the hole; make sure the animal was dead before burying them. Then cover them up with the dirt that came from the hole. He would pat the dirt with the metal flat part of the shovel. When all done, he would say this is apart of life and responsibility. We enjoy each other, the life God gives us together and when it's time to depart we give our loved ones a good resting place.

Son: Dad and mom went through a partying spell there, where dad was getting drunk on Friday nights with mom; as they went bar hopping together to every bar that had a dance floor in it. Their group of friends would go together. Dad would be so drunk that he would be crawling up the steps to go to their bed; swearing all the way up the steps, at 3:00 AM in the morning. If he didn't barf in the kitchen sink, he would barf in the second-floor toilet. Swearing off and on like a drunken sailor as they would say. I'd be lying in bed with my eyes closed, acting like I was asleep, as he crawled pass my bedroom door. This is where I learned my dad's work hard, play hard ethics. Dad wasn't a drunk. He wasn't an occasional drinker. He just got fun wasted every Friday night with mom; hopping and dancing in all the bars that two counties had. I said all that to say this. One of those nights' mom collapses on the dance floor. Dad gets his free movie sweet heart conscious after awhile. They think she just got stupid drunk, until she started to keep doing it even after when she had a little to drink. They would laugh that it didn't take much to get mom drunk. She decides to get checked out by the doctor and the results come back that she's a diabetic. Ouch. Mom loved her sugar big time. After blacking out and being emitted into the hospital, things changed around the farm house real fast. Mom learned a new diet, they both quit drinking and going to the bars. So, when dad said diabetes saved mom, it really did. She got more proactive in her church and helping unfortunate families, etc. During this change dad gave up his food group desires and ate the same foods mom did to support her. He learned how to catch mom's insulin sugar reactions in the middle of the night. Breaking out in bed soaking sweats; he was there for every one of them for the rest of her life, no matter how he felt. He was like an in-house doctor to mom.

Son: The family trip to Yellowstone National Park. Mom had this idea that in just a few years we boys will be moving on and the odds of us getting back together to do something big like this will be next to null. So, dad and mom thought of an inexpensive place we could go as a family. We've already have been to Florida a zillion times, up north and Cedar Point. They decided it was Yellowstone. Dad asked the old neighbors, who lived next to us when dad and mom were in the Small Ranch home, if we could take their trailer hitch camper with us on our trip to Yellow Stone; to keep the cost down. Dad and mom shared their A-Frame cabin with them for several weekends over the years without charging a penny. So they obliged. Next dad was pulling out the national map of the United States to plot his path to Yellowstone. Dad mentioned that there are long stretches of highway that have nothing but farm land for hundreds of miles and he was hoping I would be up to driving it, since I had just got my driver's permit. I was stoked. I would drive for a few hours; the whole family was sleeping in the car while pulling a camper. I was used to pulling dad's farm equipment behind the tractor, so this should be no different. We stayed in the national franchised camp grounds along the way there and back. Driving back was hell. I didn't want to drive but had to; so, dad and mom could get a nap in before they drove. Once inside Yellowstone, we saw Old Faithful blow, moose, chipmunks and beautiful water falls. Dad stayed by the car and camper while me, my brother and mom walked down to a raging river full of gigantic rocks. We tried sitting on them to soak our feet before making the long trip back home. One night we stayed in Yellowstone, it poured rain and the camper roof leaked. We were getting soaked so dad and mom tried to get a cabin to stay in for the night. I don't remember if we did or not. I want to say, mom and dad stayed in a cabin while at Yellowstone back in their traveling days, before having us boys. Nothing special happened during the trip, other than being together while doing something new with us boys. Dad and mom worked harmoniously together while driving, getting the camper set up and taken it down, restaurants and the need to go to bathroom during inconvenient times. No yelling, No threats. Perfect trip.

Son: After me and my brother married and moved out, Dad and mom offered their home to a man who was a Christian and wanting to change his factory job life into being a doctor. He would stay at their home so his travel time to the State University would be seriously cut down. He would go back to his home on the weekends. Mom and dad didn't charge him room and board. Every night he and dad would play pool and dad would clean his clock every time. Mean while this guy went to classes on how to play better pool. It was like for two years and then he graduated. The last night he stayed there. He was first to break the pool balls to get the game started; then he went on to clearing the table and winning the game. Dad didn't get one turn in and dad broke out laughing. Dad was really proud of this guy; they considered him a son without the bennies.

Son: After us boys left home, dad got more involve with mom in the church, by helping families in need. Dad droved his brown 84 Chevy C10 truck and volunteered to move families in need for free. They would volunteer together to serve food to the homeless at a Soup Kitchen in Flint. Mom would knit, crochet, and sew blankets with a group of church women. These would be given to the young women who decided to have their babies versus aborting them. The biggest and most memorable volunteering moment dad and mom shared together, was when making a trip to Kentucky; to take supplies to families that lived in the hills. They loaded the bus and truck up with supplies. No one had extra money to take with them on the trip, let alone gas money. They get about half way to Kentucky and the truck runs out of gas. The needle is below the E mark on the dash panel instrument. By faith they keep driving, the truck never died. It kept going until they arrived to their destination and then to a gas station. They had traveled from Michigan to Kentucky on one tank of gas. A miracle to them; especially when the gas tank held about 15 gallons of gas and the truck was getting about 18 to 20 miles a gallon. Yup. That's good for about 300 miles. The trip was 550 miles. So, the truck was driving on fumes and this miracle help bring closure to dad and mom's dark days in their relationship; while living on the 80 Acre farm.

Son: Dad and mom ended up giving their wedding bands to God; as a commitment of giving their relationship with each other in their marriage to God. It was weird at first seeing their ring fingers bare, but an awesome testimony of making a physical show of commitment, on each of their parts to each other; without saying a word to each other.

Son: There's a ton more events that took place during dad's and mom's stay on the farm, but are more related to me growing up which I elaborate in the books; *The Ten Commandments my Father Taught Me* and *The Ten Commandments My Mother Taught Me,* Including the famous horse manure shredding machine I built, dirt clod fights, vegetable and fruit stands, tree camps/forts, the pond I built, embarrassingly accidently kicking my brother out the second story bedroom window, inner tubing on the river the old school way, literally nailing the neighborhood bully, Toby diving for under water rocks; just to name a few moments while growing up in dad and mom's family. And later on, building a hydro board press with dad and testing the hydro board on river. Go to the WarriorsCreed store on Zazzle®.com if interested in purchasing their related inspirational products when available.

Son: Looking back it's neat to know dad didn't get jacked at wanting justice, accepted that the subdivision plan didn't go through and started to think about plan B. Plan B ended up being more flexible with mom's unforeseen depression and diabetes. Whereas if the subdivision plan went through, then it would have added more stress to mom's condition. Dad is once again a laid-back smoothie big picture pro.

Dad: 02-15-17. If I stayed there, I would have expanded it. I couldn't sit still. I wanted to keep moving all the time.

✝ Visiting My Dad ✝

S on: Dad would offer stopping to get ice cream, candy bars to get me to go with him, while he bought beer and chewing tobacco for his dad. He went to visit his dad maybe once or twice a month. One time, I decided to stay home. Mom asked why I didn't go with dad. I said I just wanted to stay home. Mom replied your dad enjoys you going along with him to visit his dad. I didn't know that. So, from then on, I went with dad every time.

Son: Up until a few years before dad's dad passed on; the family decided to personally take care of their dad versus putting him in an assistant living facility. Each sibling who was interested would watch their dad for one week at a time. So, about every five to six weeks dad got a chance to take care of his dad. This happened while dad and mom were in the Farm House. We were fortunate to have his dad in our home the week of his birthday. Mom made him a birthday cake and we sung Happy Birthday to him. He smiled a big smile. Extremely quiet man; didn't talk at all. I would try to start talking with him and he would just shrug his shoulders. Dad would bath his dad and mom would cook him food. It got so that they had to have him wear an adult diaper to stop him from messing in his pants. Dad had a lot of compassion for his dad. Dad mentioned his dad was a big man, big hands, big nose and big ears. When seeing them sit next to each other, it was more evident there ever.

Son: His dad never had seen a doctor for his personal health conditions throughout all his life. So, the brother in charge decided to put him the hospital over night; for testing and observation. The next day when dad and his brothers went up to hear their dad's results. The doctor said, they didn't get a chance to run any test on their dad. He kept throwing the metal bed pan at the nurses. His advice to the sons was, if your dad has lived this long without going to the doctors then let him live the way he wants. His dad drunk a lot of organic cedar, hard cider and chewed tobacco most of his adult life. He passed on in his sleep from natural causes. No cancer. No heart attack. No stroke. His wife had passed on six years before him. She reached the age of 79 yrs old. He married her when she was 16 and he was 26. There was a ten years difference between them. There's a possibility he passed on with a broken heart missing his childhood sweet heart.

Son: What did we discover on date digging? Dad's dad was born just before Thanksgiving Day 11-28 1883; on 11-23-1883. He passed on just after Thanksgiving Day 11-23-1978; on 11-27-1978. So his loved ones would be Thankful for receiving dad's dad life into this world and his loved ones would be Thankful for dad's dad life while in this world. These Thanksgiving dates to birth and passing dates are almost symmetrical. If we flipped them, it would be like he was born and died on Thanksgiving. But better yet, it was that he was born in the Spirit of the Thanksgiving Season versus the day itself. Which is a direct correlation with his life; he was a very compassionate and giving man. He gave freely to his wife, his family and his community. It was as though, it was his way of being Thankful for getting a chance to be apart of this world, all of the 95 years and four days of it.

✝ Sister-N-Law's Upstairs ✝

Dad: Didn't do much there. We were busy building our new Square Ranch home. Go out to eat. A lot of card playing. Just used as a place to sleep.

Son: His sister-in-law was mom's oldest sister. She never worked. She married three times. Never divorced; her husbands would pass away and she would wait a few years then marry another man. The men she married made enough to take care of her family. The last man she married was the man who taught her dad how to wire a home. He was the man who also taught my dad Richard how to wirer a home. And then latter he reviewed how to wire a home with me, when my dad built most of my first home. When we found this out in my mom's mom memoirs, the thought was when mom's dad got promoted to inspector at a factory in Flint; her older sister's third husband could have been an electrician working there and mom's dad met him there.

Son: Mom's oldest sister was a good penny pincher. She loves going north in the summer months and in the winter months, when her daughters can take her, she loves going to Florida to stay with her daughter in Florida. She owned a trailer in Ft Meyers; in the same Trailer Park her mom was in; as well as dad and mom later did. They spent their winters there together as a family. Mom's oldest sister lived about a mile down the road from dad and mom's 80 Acre Farm. She lived there most of her life until recently. To date of this writing, she is still alive and about 94 years old.

✝ Square Ranch ✝

S on: This is the current home that dad is living in now. He wouldn't go into any details; when I would mention some of the events but he would agree.

Son: During most of the time dad and mom lived in this ranch home, I was raising my family by myself as a single parent. I was in an out of dad's and mom's life, so these listed events are more of observation verses living in their presents; while growing up with them in their family.

Son: This was the last home; dad and mom would be living in together. They were fully enjoying the benefits of what they had attained. They knew this was the results of their committing to each other; the building their lives together, throughout all their lives. From the day they met each other at the Free Movies to now in their golden years.

Son: Dad was working in the Gas Department for a Utility Company for a few years while in the Square Ranch before retiring in 1994. He was on multiple shift schedules. A new shift began every hour to keep a fresh new crew starting every hour of the day. Brilliant on the Company's part, but rough on the workers if they got scheduled to start at a new hour. Schedules came out two weeks early so that the workers could plan their personal lives better. For being on multiple shifts this gave dad the opportunity to get really good pay; especially when the gas lines got damage some how. He was getting triple time around the clock when sent to out of town jobs. He got paid to sleep and meals were free. His last ten years at the Utility Company was better than all the other thirty years combined. No matter what shift dad was working on mom was very supportive.

Son: The Utility Company wanted to encourage their senior employees to retire, so they offered dad a buy out. The first round was less than $100,000; dad pasted. The second round was between $100,000 to $200,000; dad pasted again. The third time around; they explained to dad this was their final offer and if he doesn't take it, he won't be offered another buy out; period. So, he took it. The buy out was over $200,000. Out of the thousands of employees they employed, only a few got this offer, dad was one of them.

Son: Other than mom dealing with dad being home all day, she loved dad being retired. They had more options to enjoy their golden years together.

Son: During the first few years of dad being retired; dad and mom were eating out to different restaurants two to four nights a week with their friends, her sisters and their husbands. Going to church, volunteering, going to Florida for the winter and staying with her sister and her husband for a couple of years; until dad and mom bought their own trailer in the same park. Stay up north at the A-Frame cabin for weeks at a time, going to casinos, taking cruises. Having their 50 and 60yr Wedding Anniversary Parties; these were coordinated by my brother and his wife; they did an awesome job. And they bought two new cars with cash.

Son: As dad settled into retirement, he learned how to fly a single engine airplane. The day he was taking his final solo flying test, he talked mom in going with him. All that time he was doing the flying, mom thought it was the instructor and dad was the assistant; he did such a great job. She was then amazed and impressed how dad did it all by himself. He started the airplane, drove it down the run way, flew up into the skies around Flint and then touching it back down on the run way.

Son: After conquering flying, being a professed Christian, dad decides to unbiasly attend the local Jewish Synagogue to see how really different Jews are from Christians versus listening to Christians tell them what they think who Jews are. Brilliant on his part; mom didn't want anything to do with it. He pledges to the Rabbi that he would not witness to the members about Christ; he would just sit and observe their practices. Dad observed their Saturday Morning services and Bible Studies on Wednesday Nights. He did this for two years consistently week after week. I believe this is where he learned how to write Hebrew. He purchased a lot of Jewish Books they referenced to. His conclusion; there is no difference between Christians and Jews. They are one in the same, except for the name they give their Messiah.

Son: As dad's retirement kicks in; both dad's and mom's siblings and the spouses are starting to pass on. As they started to pass away, so did their hanging out with each. One family after the other, dad and mom were going to their funerals until they're almost the only ones living. The siblings that are still alive, they are so much older than dad and mom, their health issues are preventing them from getting together regularly. Dad and mom were both the youngest ones, born in both their families.

Son: In the midst of dad's and mom's siblings passing on, mom has a quad bypass about ten years before she passed on. Dad and mom didn't know they were about to be blessed with a longer life together, when mom slipped and fell on the hospital entrance floor. It bummed her knee up really bad. Dad and mom were visiting her sister's husband in the hospital and on their way out she slipped. Mom was emitted to the same hospital shortly afterwards because of it. While she was recovering in the hospital, they ran test on her and found out they needed to operate on her heart

ASAP. She needed a quad bypass now; but couldn't because of her knee was in unstable condition. They kept close eye on her and was waiting as long as they could in hopes her knee would heal up strong enough to handle quad bypass surgery. Mom talked about being at peace with everything. The real kicker was when she got to go home and recoup there. Dad stepped up in helping mom heal faster. During that process, mom broke down and cried, talked about how she has taken dad for granite all those years. She was blessed to have him, be there in her life all those years.

Son: A couple of year's later dad had his bypass. He was in a Sunday Morning Service at my brother's church, when he started to complain about being in pain around his chest area. My brother insisted that dad should go to the hospital now, but dad didn't want to. It was either just after church or after coming home from church, dad decides to go to the hospital. Once there, after a few tests he was emitted same day; for bypass surgery. Once into surgery dad says he remembers the doctor putting his pumping heart on his chest. As the doctors were performing surgery on dad, he says he was looking at his heart pumping on his chest. After he's sent home to heal the rest of the way, dad would say; if the doctor tells me I can't mow the yard anymore I'm going to mow the yard anyways, even if I die. At least I died doing something I wanted to do; before I died. He'd laugh.

Son: After mom's bypass she realizes she needed to appreciate dad more. And after dad's bypass he realizes he's at peace with what he has experienced and accomplished in his life.

Son: Dad and mom go on to updating their bath room tub shower into a walk-in shower. Update the septic field to the A-Frame Cabin. My brother financed these Cabin updates, of which dad paid him back in the winter of 2016-17. They do everything they can think of in making their lives easier incase their health deteriorates; one of them might be able to take care of the other one, while still in their home.

Son: Dad starts to mention he can't make the long trips to Florida by car and he's not interested in flying to Florida. He says he's done traveling unless he has too.

Son: Dad and mom stop going to church, volunteering and are contented in living in their home without always doing something. Mom stops sewing. Dad takes longer at doing small projects but most of all, he enjoys being with mom all the time, knowing if the Koreas didn't declare peace, he wouldn't have had this life with her.

☦ Our Florida Trailer ☦

S on: 03-07-17. This chapter was put in this book at the tail end of almost having it completely written. I didn't get in dad's home more than five minutes and he says he found all these tickets and pictures; he couldn't remember where they came from. So, as I started looking through them. The pictures were of their trailer they bought in Florida, to have a place to stay while being in Florida. The trailer park was the same one that mom's mother lived in after her husband pasted away on March 7, 1964. I just looked up this date while writing this in the early morning hours of 03-08-17. Dang, this is fate. I'm getting goose bumps. Need to stop and absorb this connection that dad had yesterday being the death anniversary date of his father-in-law; my grandpa. Wow. That's exactly 53 yrs later to the date. And that's the year mom and dad got married in; 1953. Double goose bumps.

Son: Dad's Mother-in-Law's Memoirs, mentions that she might have had TB when she was 13. Her mother took her to Florida and stayed in for three to four months; until she was healed up. It was common practice to send children to Sun Camps to be healed of TB. The children would stay outside and the "Sun" bath with only their shorts and or bathing suits/t-shirts on. I believe this might of have been the connection mom's mother had in obtaining her desire to live in Florida part of the year and then later in her life, permanently.

Son: Dad's Mother and Father-in-Law fell in love with Florida and had the intent; to having a place to live there in the winter months and live at their Cabin home up north Michigan.

Son: After her husband's passing, she went ahead and followed through on their plans. This appears to be the catalysts that got her four daughters including mom to go to Florida for winter vacations with their families. Mom and dad got so addicted in going to Florida, year after year. Before us boys were born and for at least seven years straight after I was born. As we got older, dad and mom would go down by themselves. When we boys were of age to be by ourselves, we had to take care of ourselves for a week. They would usually leave on a Thursday - Friday morning after we got on the school bus, then to the following Wednesday night.

Son: Dad and mom really started showing their love in going to Florida together; after dad retired. They bought a trailer in a Florida trailer park, fixed it up; went there every winter until dad decided he didn't want to drive the long distance anymore. That last year they went to Florida, they had their trailer sold to two twin sisters before leaving for the last time to come home to Michigan.

✝ My Ancestry ✝

S on: This is a real shame that we can't publish linage of my dad's ancestry due to privacy rights of the individuals related to dad's pass; especially for my children's future reference. But that will be another book at a later date. For now, we will go over the general bullet points.

Son: Shortly after dad retired, he and mom got real interested in Dad's Ancestry. Dad's last name as a person's last name is a unique. It's not as common as Jones, Smith, etc. So, if you ever meet someone with the dad's last name, they are related to my dad.

Son: He found out Dad's original last name starts around the early 1800's with Dad's Great Grandfather was born in Canada on Oct 19, **1823** or 1824, and might have died in Michigan. He married a woman who was born in England. It appears that it might have been a personal decision to change our original last name to the last name my dad has now; when in and or when might of migrated from Canada. Dad's Great Grandfather had Dad's Grandfather in **1852** and he died in 1923. He was in and or migrated to Michigan. Dad's Grandfather had his dad in **1883** and he died in 1975. Dad's dad out lived all his siblings. Most of his dad's siblings died in their twenties; leaving dad's dad sole heir of his father's assets. My dad was born in **1932**. My dad had me in **1960**. I had my son in **1986**. And my son had his son in **2011**. This is seven generations spanning almost 200 years.

Son: Shortly after dad retired, he was driven to starting back up his Family's Reunions.

Son: After his mother passed on, the Family Reunions came to a screeching halt. As time went on, Dad went to each of his siblings and tried to talk them into having a Family Reunion. No one was interested.

Son: Dad and mom decided do the family reunion themselves at a local city park. Moms built a mailing address list of know relatives around the state of Michigan then invited them to the family reunion. Dad got three ice cream hand cranking mixers working and ready for the reunion. The kids loved making home made cranked ice cream from scratch. The reunions were a success, thanks to dad and mom's efforts in making everyone feel welcome and part of the family.

Son: After a few years' dad made the announcement that him and mom were getting too old for this and the younger women should take over if their still interested in keeping the Family Reunions alive. It worked for a few more years; but as more of dad's siblings past on and or health reasons, stopped the Family Reunions from continuing on. If they are still going on, I am unaware of it. I don't remember getting any invitations in the last few years. Gags. I should know these things. Oops.

Son: Mom eventually attained Family addresses from other states and contacted them to see if they had any information on the family ancestry. One or two of them respond and kept in contact over years; thanks to mom's dedication in helping dad find his ancestry

Son: Recap. Dad's desire to restart the family reunions leads dad and mom to researching dad's ancestry.

✝ My Wife's Passing ✝

S on: Mom passed on Tuesday 07-07-15 in the early
afternoon in the hospital room, where she was being
waited on.

Son: That January before mom passed, her body was
starting to retain fluids. I didn't know it, but dad refers to
it in the June just before mom's passing. Mom did make
comments about how she's gaining weight and should start
exercising. Mom loved her sugar and was using her higher
doses of insulin to cover it up. I called her out on it back in
2008 when my pituitary gland enlarged and I needed to start
taking insulin. In my mind I thought bullshit. I will watch my
sugar levels before I eat versus after I eat. Dad would make
a peaceful comment about this from time to time to mom.
But it was her life; she can live it the way she wants. Sure
enough after a couple of months of testing myself, I proved
to the doctor my sugar was in range and didn't need insulin.

Son: That June before mom's passing, she started to have
an occasional cough. The family run preventive medicine
center, that mom and dad was going to over the last twenty
plus years, was now being ran by the second generation.
Whatever was being prescribed didn't get rid of her cough.
The different prescriptions seemed not to be working. Mom
was starting to cut dad's conversations off. At times dad
couldn't even start a sentence and she would cut him off.
She was adamant about letting me know how dad was losing
his mind and forgetting all the time. But so was she. She
would forget her sun glasses at their up north cabin and dad

would turn around to go back and get them; keys and other things. That day she was driven not to let dad talk period, I spoke up and said it would be great just to listen to my dad finish his own thoughts, in his own words. At that moment, I got these overwhelming thoughts, that sometime this year, the family was only going to be hearing dad talk and mom was going to be the one listening. Mom got pissed, went into the fire place room and started to pout. I said, mom why do you always have to have the center of attention? Dad, spoke up and said we're lucky to have mom around, we should be thankful. Mom went on to say, when they were up north the last time, it was around the midnight hour and she couldn't sleep. Her last try, was trying to fall asleep sitting up in the brown crush velvet recliner, in the cabin's living room. Finally, she closed her eyes and for a moment she was at perfect peace. She said it was the most perfect peace she had experienced, since being in her coma while living in the farm house with dad. She said it felt so good that she didn't want to wake up; she knew if she felt asleep, she wasn't going to be waking up. Just as she was about to let go, she heard a voice saying, "Why do you want to stay here?" She said, "I want to stay here to help Richard". She immediately woke up and told dad they need to go back to their Flint home. She didn't tell dad what just happened. As their getting on the highway, dad gets on the wrong entrance ramp to head home. Mom gets frustrated and asks dad is he ok and is it too late to be driving. Dad says to her, "Its ok. I'll turn around and that I'm here for you". At that moment mom knew it was the right thing to do and told dad about her experience while trying to sleep in the brown crush velvet recliner.

Son: The evening before mom's passing, you could see mom was having a hard time coping. Sitting in the chair trying to sleep and not being able to sleep long enough; to get rest she needed for days. Dad was going to the drug store to get a new upgraded prescription. I decided to stay while dad was gone just in case something happened to mom or she needed something. She kept nodding off for a few seconds then break the nod with a cough; a soft cough. She would awaken and begin to talk about what she learned while watching the television the night before; with photo graphic clarity. If I had closed my eyes and just listened to her talk, I would have thought nothing was wrong with her. I sat quietly when she would start to nod off as she was talking. This kept going on until Dad got back from waiting for mom's prescription to be filled. It felt like forty-five minutes to an hour. I let mom know dad had just pulled up into the car port and that I would be leaving, long day.

Son: On Tuesday the 07-07-15. I did my normal routine of taking Max, my pit bull for a walk, then over to mom and dads to check up on them. I have been really fortunate to live a couple of city blocks from them for the last fifteen plus years of my life. Now I'm at dad's glass see through storm door, seeing dad sitting at the "modern" solid oak kitchen table, they bought together in the late 1950's. He looked like he was in deep thought. He's not getting up to unlock the storm door. I check it and its not locked. I go in and sit at the table. He doesn't say a word. I hear no sounds of mom in the house, so I automatically assumed the new prescription medicine dad bought yesterday was working. Mom was finally sleeping. To break the silence, I ask dad how mom's doing. He says with a sobering vegetative look on his face, "mom didn't make it". They tried to bring her back, it didn't work. She's gone. I now had that sobering vegetative look on dad's face saturating my whole being. Totally shocked. She was talking so clear, her memory was sharp as a whip, and last night was going to be the last conversation I had with my mother. At that point, I'm so glad I made the decision to stop to check up on them, to stay while dad went to get the prescription. And sitting their quietly so that my mom could fall asleep. Dad and I sat there in silence for about a half hour or so. He was soberly trying to absorb the fact that his free movie sweet heart was gone. I sat there and man boy cried off and on, while in shock.

Son: Looking at the clock, I said to dad we need to start calling people to let them know, before it gets too late. Is it ok to look through mom's ph and ph book to get numbers to call? He said ok. When I picked up mom's ph, it had a text message on it and she forgot or couldn't press the send button, earlier that day. Then time associated with the text message to me was around 9:00am. It said, "New medicine isn't working. Going straight to the hospital instead of doctors...." My being in shock relapsed again. I'm thinking wow, if she would of press the send key, I would have known that they were in the hospital that day and dad's news would have had a different affect on me. In her last moments she was still trying to reach out.

Son: I called my brother first and was hoping he would be there in time to help make the arrangements. Then we started to call her nieces and nephews of her past on siblings. Her oldest sister was the only one still alive. She is the oldest of the four sisters and still alive. I called the funeral home, the local city newspaper. I had moments of silence, sniffles and wiping my eyes and nose with facial tissues in between. Dad still in shock. We've must have gotten up, perhaps hugged? But when we sat down, we were now in each others chairs. Call after call, some leaving voice mails, others I was listening to her loved ones in shock and wanted to know when the funeral was so they can make arrangements; to send flowers and or be there.

Son: I made most of the upfront arrangements, notices in the local city newspaper and appointment time with the funeral director; the basic un-financial decisions to get the funeral rolling.

Son: The funeral came and went in a big blur. Dad never broke down and cried. He looked like he was thinking a lot. He had a sober, shocked and surreal look on his face.

Son: The highlights of her funeral from my part of the experience were of the following:

Son: My children were very supportive and did what they could. My son and his family live out of state. He thought instead of rushing around and making arrangements to be here for the funeral it would be best to spend a few days having personal time with his grandpa a few months after the funeral. Later it proved to be a good move on his part.

Son: My mother's oldest sister, on the morning just before mom's funeral told me a story, I longed forgot. She skipped school to go see her new little baby sister (mom) at the hospital the day she was born into this world. When done with her story, I looked into her eyes, thanked her for being here on the day that her little sister was leaving this world. God give her strength to be there for her grand children when they need her.

Son: All through mom's funeral, dad was quiet. When he did talk, he said a few brief words.

Son: A lot of support for mom's passing; her friends and family out of state; stopped what they were doing and spent a couple days in Michigan. Mom would have been happy: an elder from her mother's side showed up, I believe her maid of honor showed up. She might have been just her best friend. Church friends from the last church mom and dad were attending. Her pastor did her benediction and committal services. He did a perfect job in listening and articulating the bullet points of her life to those who attended her funeral services. A lot of dad's side of the family showed up in support of dad. Her nieces and nephews showed up on mom's dad side of her family. Most of her grandchildren from my family showed up.

✠ My Wife's Memoirs ✠

D ad: My wife's memoirs on how we met.
Son: These are mom's words, written below as she wrote them on a pad of paper. Some of the words are misspelled, some run-on sentences and some sentences didn't make sense. These spelling errors were intentionally left in; to keep this copy of her memoirs, in her original writing.

Son: Most of the thoughts were continuous on the pad, so for reading purposes we separated the change in thoughts, with one line of space.

Son: Then for rights of privacy we had to replace people's names with a generic substitute. Again, it's too bad, but understandable on their part.

My wife, born 4/4/35, Flint. Parents: – Name & Name. Sisters, Name, Name, & Name-

Our home on Street Name had a lot of big apple trees.

In the back of property, we had a bldg that was used for storing coal in the winter & in summer, used as a play house –

Near the back of the bldg, was a large old tree that had a huge low branch, extending a good warp out. I got I loved climbing out on it. Spent many hours in that tree, I could look out over the fields, watch the animals, see the birds, listen to all the sounds. Mother would have to call me out for lunch and as soon as I could get away, back up the tree I would go.

Thru all my tree climbing, a nail was in one, drove it thru my right knee, leaving a scar and another time, w different tree, but a nail, hit my front baby tooth and knocked it out –

Named Uncle.

We had to dogs, a black cocker, called Rex and a white & black spotted hound called Sport – Dad was a hunter, so the hound was used for hunting phesants, rabbits, geese & spectal, gray pat? Rex became our house pet – when dogs were young, they were kept outside –

Fur each dog. Dad stingen a wier from / tree to another – and hooked a chain to dog collar and attached to wreir – alouding freedom to run back & forth –

During the cold winter, Dad would make corn meal in a large kettle and let cool, slice and feed to dogs. They would goble it down. Dad said, it would put weigh on them and would help keep them warm –

Mother wasn't affectiate, if I hugged her 1st she would return it but Dad was the 1st to reach out – I enjoyed sitting on his lap and running my hands thru his hair – If I ever got injured, like the nail cutting my leg, falling, he would be sure to clean, put medicine & bandage put on correctly along with a kiss and tell me everything would be ok. If dad wasn't around then mother would hurry, slap on bandage and send me on my Dad got home and look at it, he would do it all over making sure no infection would come to me –

Mom was a protector, I got mad one time slammed the kitchen door and the glass fall out and broke in fine pieces – She made me clean it up & said if I would promise her that

I wouldn't do it again, she would tell Dad the wind blow ~~it out~~ "?" stuck. So, of course, I promised and from that experience, when I got mad I made sure nothing got broken.

Dad was the discipliner, Sometime sisters would get in a pillow fight and Dad would call out & give warning & of course, it wouldn't be hedded he'd come in the room, take his belt off, line, Name, Name, Name, up and spams them. I would be in corner afraid, and learning what not to do to get to afford trouble – 3 times & watch out. This was pass down in raising Name & Name.

Once a week My folks along with us kids, would go out, after supper to visit Grandma Name in City. (Road Name) Name Rd. was then 2 lanes, cement highway with trees planted on both sides. It was beautiful, the tree branches reach out to each other and looking down thru them was life go thru a tunnel – eventually, the county cut them down because of deaths caused by hitting trees.

I was real young when Grandpa Name died, *(estimate 29 yrs old)* don't remember his face but remember he's right hand. He would put a penny in his hand closed and I would try in lift each finger, I'd get 1 finger open be working on the other and he'd closed the one I got open. This went on all the time until Dad was ready to leave Then he was leave them open and I'd get that penny – Little did I know he was teaching me perseverance –

Going out to City Name was ritual – Mother loved the Family Name, they would partly a lot, drank, smoke, cussed, told dirty stories and played cards –

The holidays, would go to Aunt Name and Uncle Name – They were the only ones that had a finished basement and had room for all of us – I remember, getting real bored, wanted to go home, would end up laying down and going to sleep –

go back to front

Cousin Name (Nic Name) Last Name, lived to the left of our house and he would come over & play with me. Aunt Name, would watch over him light a halk –

I was given a childs doctor & nurse set – so I had Name, laying down in one of our beds, taking his temperture, looking at his tongue – When Aunt Name came thunter in, gerabed Bill up, said, something to me, which at my age didn't understand and you guess there wasn't playing nurse anymore – Mother was laughing and told me never mine what she said – which to this day I don't remember – but can imiganion, ha

Another, time, with Aunt Name, I came home crying, She & Uncle Name accused me of chasing after their chickens with a stick, which I didn't do from that point on I saw both of them, minn, and was glad they moved. It took years to eraser that experience, I almost forgot it, but, later in life got very close to both of them and she got to laughing one day, and told me – again the story Uncle Name was a gentle, slow, speaking man and confest to me, that hes received the Lord Jesus into his heart about 8 weeks to his death – Aunt Name, received Jesus, a few months after his death –

Time passes, in "2003?" My husband and I were having lunch with cousin, Name & Name Last Name, when, he confests to me, that he was the one that done it and he told his folks that I did it - And that he never did tell them. So in summing up this story, see the effects of a lie –

Around the age of 7, the school was closing down for 3 days Easter and I decided I wanted to go to church, Mother, made me a new dress and bought me black patient shoes – I walked down wo to the church in the Woods, Church Name, on Name Rd They took me down in the basement to the Sunday school class – I remember just a little of the story of Jesus but they gave me a bible & a picture of Jesus with children – I kept them for many a year. Losted years later

Going into my school years, I started kintalgarden, in Name School, School was across from Grandma Last Name and when I had to go full time, at lunch hour, I would go over to Grandma's and sit under one of her large trees in the front yard – looking from her house, facing east, on right side, she had cherry trees, you can guess I'd like to climb – on left side she had her flowers, large purple & yellow Iris, Big deep pink, wine peonias – Later, Oldest Sister, was given some and she gave My Other Sister some and than I got some from Her – There in my front yard today 8/8/08 –

In Mother's memoirs, she tells about selling our home and moving to City Name – when that happen, I was heart broken, and made it known to them – My 2nd Oldest Sister was going to stay with Grandma Last Name to finish up her Senior year so Mother, also, maded arrangements for me to stay – They paid her room & food for both of us. We would go home on weekends –

Grandma Last Name, as mother said, wasn't very affectiate and she had rules – In to bed by 9:00pm. She listened to her radio stations. She played satary but never played cards with me – Grandma, was blind in left eye due to caterat, a frosty cover over left eye glasses – She had a dairy she wrote in every day – I learned my table manners from her, she place side dish for fruit, salads, silverware in proper place – if I wanted a piece of bread, I was to cut it in ½ because she said I was not to waste food but if I still wanted more, than I could have it. She taught me to say, please & thank you – Well, 3 weeks of instruction, home sick, & I had tried out for the lending part in my 5th grade christmas play and lost out to my best friend, Name Last Name – I so dispointed, and told the folks I was ready to be a country girl (I didn't no at the time we were country there).

Oh, regarding, learning. I had difficulty in reading, the state had removed phonic and go to picture association – more memory – which has pleged me all these years – My average was usually C's – When entering the country school known as the "English School" located on corner of Road Name & Name Rd – It went up to 7 grades, I was still in 5th and there were 3 of us – That is where I received most of my learning – because she would work with lower grades and I would take it all in – My 7th year, I had ended up with mostly all A's – (and only student) They closed the school and consolidated with School Name – Returning to where I originally – started – Marks ending up with B & C's –

Son: The last school mom and dad went to, each of their different schools merged together; bringing mom and dad together. This last school was financed by mom's mother side of the family. I believe mom said it was completely paid for by her mother's family side. At one time her mother's side of the family owned all the farm land for about six to seven miles long the same road. They named the road after her mother's side of the family.

In the English School, my friends, were Name Last Name and his sister Name – Their folks were musically inclined, Mother Name, played panio and father Name played Voilin, and weekend played for Square Dances – They, also, played a month on Saturday raising money for English School – Dad & Mother loved dancing, so that's how I became a dancer too – The Last Name took a real liking of me, so they would drove over and pick me up every Sat and I'd go with them – I just loved being with them, my folks, were getting older Dad was Aged sleeping alot after getting home from work (I realize now, why he was tryed he stayed up all hours) – weekend, after they got the cabin, up north, they would drive up there, play cards way into the night – Come back Sundays late and up early to go to work

Regarding, the cabin life, weekends were ritual and during summer enjoyed the water – would go and gather frogs, Dad built me a wire pen and I would gather water weeds for their food, caught bugs, anything I tought they'd eat – The shore line of the river wasn't very good, 2 to 3 feet an it would drop right off into the deep – Mother would watch me but as time and years elapsed she eased up. I began to adventure and found out one day I was swimming and it was easy and I loved it – So my sports was swimming – At the time, the river, had logs, so would swim to one, rest, and move on – ending at the Store, a mile from the cabin – Had our dog, Rex as a play competion – He loved the water, and would ride up front in fishing boat.

There was an incident, probably, in the 1st year in moving into cabin – Dad had Sister's Name & I raking up leave on front hill leaning to river – We hit a nest of bees and they began to swarm around and in fear started running for cabin. Sister's Name know enough to run long side of cabin, cut corner quick an they flu by – Not me I ran right into cabin, bring bees with me – Dad went to killing them and Mother, shook them out of my hair – I ended up with 2 bites, Mary none.

In my freshman year, I had a school bus friend Name Last Name, several times, come up north – I see her occasional over the years and she shared about how much fun she had at our place, liked my parents - . That her home life wasn't very good - Name received Jesus as "Lord and shared she had many wounds healed but good memory about us.

When about age 13, during summer, City Name had outside movies, Friday Nights, so Dad & Mother would go see Grandma Last Name and they would let me go up town to the movies. Second Oldest Sister was going with Name Last Name and she told me, his cousin, Richard Last Name was near my age and probably would be there. So, meeting with friends, walking down street, I got introduced to

Richard – Later, he came over, on Motoroyelme? with Name Last Name. Between Name & Him, they were really trying <u>too</u> <u>impress</u> –

Meantime, I'm running with the Last Name and he showed up, again, when I'm 14. I ask my mother, if I could date, she said, she'd talk it over with Dad – Dad wasn't sure, but Second Oldest Sister, went to bat and talked them into it. Telling them he came from a good family – So, Richard, slowly became part of family – Dad had chain falls hanging in the tree, used to lift cars to work on – My father told him on his 1st visit, you better not lay a hand on her, Do you see those chains, that's where you'll hanging – Dad appear real hard, but, soft inside –

We dated 4 years, went to movies and Saturday Nights, went Square Dance held in the old Name Hall, on Name Rd

Name & Name Last Name played in band – Name told me, years later, that they had high hopes of me marrying their son, Name and when they seen me with Richard, it was hard to swallow –

After putting Mother's (My Mother's Name) memoirs together – I realized that Name was like Name to Mother - <u>Only</u> good friends –

Richard had quit school to help his Dad on farm – Worked in Apple Orchard, when he came to see me, he either drove the farm Ford Truck or his brothers car – My Dad was getting a new car and offered to sell the 1948 Desota to Richard ($500). Because of his age and having nothing of value, couldn't get a loan – My father needed money to put on his car. Richard ask his Dad & he said no so went to Bro Name. And he gave us what we needed – The agreement was to pay off 1 yr plus interest 6%. Richard, age 19, decided to vituer into a Floral business named "Dick Florest." It was located on Name Rd. The building, glass panels, and boiler were in awful shape so agreement with owner was to make repairs for 1 year rent free – Took over in fall & worked daily, opened up for business at Christmas – Sold Christmas trees & poinetta's. and planted Lilies for Easter season – and gladions for summer along with garden plants – When year came to end, sold everything and cleared $650.00. With that, he propose and bought my engagement ring -

Son: There was one partial sentence written after this but erased and hard to see, so it wasn't added.

Son: Mother was a good speller. She taught me short cuts in solving math problems and finding topic sentences in paragraphs. When writing her memoirs into this book, I broke down and cried, seeing a glimpse into her childhood. I never really mourned mother's passing. It was too fast, my brother was even faster in trying to take dad to Out of State Name. Since that backed fired, he moved aggressively into trying to put Dad into an Assistant Living Facility.

Son: Writing this book has assisted me in coming to grips and closure with my mom's passing. I love you mom and wished I had read this along time ago. I can hear you telling me this yourself in your own voice.

Son: Thank you for being moved enough to pen this account of your life in how you met dad. It cements you and dad's love story into being more inspiring than ever. Hope to see you and dad's story in the movies some day! *Come on mom,* you know it would be fitting, since you and dad's story started at the movies, it should end with you two in the movies!

✝ My Mother-in-Law's Memoirs ✝

As dictated to her daughter; my wife.

S on: Mom's mother's Real Name was referred to often by her nick name. The following events and times are mixed and given as remembered.

Son: My mother's memoirs cover her life with very little mention of details about her children as they grew up and later met their companions. This reference copy will glean out the bullet points that help crafted my mother's life and how she met my dad.

- Name Middle Name Last Name born 7/4/1901; City Name, Michigan, on a farm of which later burnt down. Her parents then moved to Road Name on the Last Name Farm. Grandpa Last Name had two farms that covered as long as the Name Rd length is today. When Grandpa died, my parents inherited the farm located on Road Name.

- During winter, Last Name folks and all the other farm families would take turns going to each others homes, with their sleighs, to a different home each week. Each week; played cards, have dinner and dance until 4 am and charged 50 cents each. Accumulated funds over the winter and in the spring would rent a hall in Flint on Name St, over the 5 & 10 cent store. Held dance, restaurant down stairs and enjoyed the water fountain on Name Street.

- Many trips to Flint with Cutter. My mother would warm soap stone in oven and put in Cutter to warm our feet.

- My mother churned butter, separated cream from milk and let sour to make cottage cheese. My mother would put newspapers on the basement floor and read them while churning to pass the time. She took butter and eggs to Flint to sell to buy other groceries and my favorite ring bologna.

- My mother would cure meat, pour fat in big crocks, took cooked lean meat on a coal cook stove in kitchen and load meat on fat. Cover meat with fat, layer after layer. This kept the meat from spoiling; would keep in cold basement.

- Remember an old tamp coming to our house, name Name Last Name. A little skinny guy lived in shack in back woods. He came quite often to the house for food. He always asked for lobber milk and bread. Taking out his dirty hanker chief and stretch it over his plate and we all secretly laughed. Dad, after milking cows, would take him to end of farm and he would walk on back to his place.

- When I was young, mother told me I was timid and quiet and my cousin Name was more active, out doors type. Name and I got into a fight. Name came running in with blood down her face and said Name hit her with her doll. My mother said, it's about time My Daughter stood up for herself. Name you got what you handed out.

- When I was thirteen, I became sick. I'm not sure, but could of have had TB. Mother took me to Florida and stayed in City Name three to four months. I believe now, it might have been pneumonia because I regained my health and we returned home.

- The doctors would check the school children. If they had TB, their families would send them to Health Camp. The Health Camps would have children dress only in their shorts and have them be in the sun all day. After about three months the children would be healed.

- My school years, I went thru Eight Grade. The school was across the street. It was a wood frame house. I was good in school and like spelling.

- About the age of seventeen, my folks let me date. Dated and danced a lot. I went to Flint Park Name Pavilion and danced all evening.

- My sister Name lived in City Name. I'd go see her and that's how I's see the Last Name, but not My Future Husband. One night attending the Sadie Hawkins dance. On Feb 29th Leap Year the women would choose their men. Name and I were dancing. My Future Husband was dancing with sister Name. When the music stop, we started up a conversation and My Future Husband asked me to dance. He remarked that he had escaped and it would be another four years before getting caught. My reply, "Oh, your going to make me wait?" He left his girl friend and came over when he saw I was alone and ask me if he could bring me coffee. I told him I don't drink it. Then he asked me if he could come over and see me and go to the fair.

- The next day, some kids came along and aske me to go with them to the fair, so I did. I wasn't there when My Future Husband came. I stood him up. So he waited and visited with my dad. He came back the next day and took my mother and I to the fair. My dad said he's the guy for you.

- We went to a lot of dances and seemed like I'd go dame with different men and My Future Husband would dance with different women. On the way home we would fight. Like playing the game, seemed we both like doing it. I liked My Future Husband's fire-spirit. He wouldn't let me get away with anything.

- We went together for about one and a half years; and married on May 31, 1919. We were supposed to be married at the Name church on Road Name in Flint. Got near city limits and car broke down. Fortunately near Rev Last Name's residence. He gave My Husband his cover-alls so he could repair car but decided to have it taken to a shop. So meantime, had pictures taken. My brother Name and wife to be, Name Last Name was our best man and maid of honor. We didn't get to the church, but Rev Last Name married us anyways.

- Our first home was in City Name on corner where it use to be a drug store, changed to grocery store and later changed to a house; lived there about a year. Moved to Flint on Name St; lived there a short time. Moved to Name St to an apartment upstairs; My Husband worked in a Garage as a repair man. From Name St moved back to Name St into a modern house. The owners sold it after we were there four months. We moved to Name St, in a house rented from Name Hospital that wasn't modern; stayed there two years. Moved to Name St, modern and lovely, but in an area where stealing went on. Moved to Name Rd, rented a very nice home. In 1927 moved to Name St. My Husband's job changed to inspector, dress up job. Car Company Name closed their shop and My Husband was released. My Husband started up a garage on Name St. This was during the Great Depression. My father died March 4th 1928, I received five lots; we were to pay back taxes but it was set for a period of years. Since My Husband didn't have good income we lost the home and in 1933 moved to Name Street. Didn't stay there long because of the smoky stove; moved from there to Street Name. My Husband closed his garage and went to work for New Car Company Name. In 1934 the shop decided to strike. (Son: Up to now, moved 10 times in 12 yr period). Name Street had an extra room that we rented it out for $4.00 a week to help pay for our rent.

- Because of unemployment we wasn't able to have any Christmas, but My Husband was called back to work Jan 1935, so we borrowed money from the Last Name's. We used the money to buy gifts and tickets for the New Year's Eve dance. My Husband decided to go to Name Brand Hardware Store Name and bought an old stub of a tree. He drilled holes in it to hold branches taken from other trees and ended up beautiful. I decorated it from what we had from previous Christmas.

- We went dancing on New Years Eve of 1935, celebrating My Husband's returning to work; at that time I was pregnant with Last Daughter's Name. She was born 4/4/1935, at home. I had women in to help me. She took longer to deliver, but very healthy. I didn't have a name for her and My Husbands sister Name was living with us, so she was the one to come up with the name, Last Daughter's Name.

- While renters would come and go with their hardships, My Husband was building our new home on Name Road from the old barn and house for $30.00. My Husband carefully took the siding, wood roofing, shingles, stone and bricks from old chimney; saved everything we could to use it to build the garage first. Ran out of money; so made the garage into our home by adding wings onto it. Too finish the inside of our home we had to borrow $500 from Name Last Name.

- First Daughter, Second Daughter and Fourth Daughter came down with Scarlet Fever and were quarantined to the house (no one left the house). My Husband took the back building, which was built to store coal in the winter and in the spring the girls would use it for a playhouse. My Husband couldn't enter the house until the girls were better.

- In 1950, we decided to build a new home at Street Number Street Name, using all new material. My Husband built, wired, plumbed and put in all the cupboards. It had a basement, 2 bedrooms, kitchen and living room; moved in 1951.

- My Fourth Daughter married in 1953 to Richard Last Name who went to the Korean Conflict; just after married.

- After My Husband had a heart attack, he took early retirement from Name Brand Car Company Name.

- In 1963, we purchased a travel trailer and went to City Name, Florida

- Before My Husband passed away, we decided we would buy a house trailer in the park in City Name and come down for the winters. So after My Husband's death, I purchased a house trailer in a trailer park in City Name FL and continued to go down in the winters. I owned and moved five times within the same park. I would move into the new trailer I bought, then rent out the older trailers; which would paid for my own rent.

Son: The following series of events were noted by my mother; dad's wife.

- Eventually My Mother sold her place in City Name Michigan and City Name Florida became her permanent home.

- The winter My Mother died, 12/15/1988, My Oldest Sister arrived at her place and made arrangements to take My Mother to the doctor's. While sitting in doctor's office, My Mother had a heart attack and put her immediately in hospital. The hospital released her; My Oldest Sister took her back to My Mother's trailer. When My Mother went to her bedroom to get some money, she fell over on the bed and died.

- There was nothing they could do for My Mother so My Oldest Sister flew her home and her funeral was held at Name Funeral Home, City Name Michigan. My Mother was buried along side of My Father in Cemetery Name, City Name MI

- Surviving daughters: Oldest Sister's Name, Second Oldest Sister's name, Third Oldest Sister's name and My Name.

☦ Mourning My Free Movie Sweet Heart ☦

S on: This last Valentine's Day 02-14-17, after asking Dad a few sober questions with sensitivity to mom's passing, he made a few statements with clarity and closure tones to them. Like someone stating a mission statement with passion. To appreciate his statements more, like I did the day he said them, we decided to put his statements at the end of this chapter

Son: Five people were about to make dad's mourning time of losing the love of his life; into a living Hell. These people would probably argue different; but I was the only one who saw the effects of their self-imposed decisions on Dad.

Son: Details omitted so that dad's story could get published.

Son: Dad said it wasn't worth holding the rest of his story up to getting most of it published. Time exposes all truth. So, the areas that are in question, we will be deleting and just noting the deleted parts with… "Details omitted." Make Sense? Good dad's life story and manuscript has gone through enough hell as it is. They say the third time is a charm. Let's see if it is. Ok, back to dad's story.

Son: Dad was about to be overwhelm with the reality that his wife was no longer going to be apart of his daily life routines.

Son: I would continue to check up on dad every two to three days. He showed signs of moving on but he had his bad days. He was a man of few words and mostly all action, so his mourning was showing up in his actions of his wife's passing; with no tears.

Son: It appears that Dad had a bad fall incident, but couldn't remember if he did or didn't. It had shaken him up enough; for him to keep insisting me and my brother to work together.

Son: I had a bad feeling it wasn't going to be good, so I called my son and told him what was going on. And if he wanted to see his grandpa, that this might be the best time and maybe his last time. My son was able to make last minute arrangements and b lined it to Flint, a few days earlier than planned.

Son: If I hadn't notified my son on my hunch, my son would have wasted all that time and expense, driving all those miles and hours with a previous neck injury pain, just to find out his grandpa was taken out of state.

Son: Dad got into wanting to split everything up. He would say, I've lived a full life and I want to make sure you get some of my belongings.

Son: So, I would say to dad, what do you think about going out of state? He said he didn't want to go. I said you're going to have to tell them that, yourself. If you don't speak up, you are and we might not ever see each other again. I was helpless not having POA's.

Son: The night before dad was being shipped out of state against his will; they were trying to convince dad, me and my middle daughter that it was in dads best interested to go out of state. I told dad he'll have to speak up for himself. When he did, dad said that he would like to go out of state;

as a vacation and not to stay there. They spoke up and said you might end up liking it there and wanting to stay. Dad said, no. His home is here in Flint and this is where he wants to be. I hug dad and told him I love him and it is and was a privilege being his son. I hugged him as though it was my last.

Son: My son and daughters took turns hanging out with dad and hugged him as it was their last too.

Son: They did end up keeping him there as long as they could. It was about two months. Once dad's urinary track infection was cured, he started to give them hell. So much so, that they packed dad up and brought him back to Flint.

Son: Dad was happy to be home. When they left, dad would say I want to stay in my own home. Why can't I. I told dad that I didn't have the POA. Dad wanted a new lawyer and new doctor; he kept asking me to get him new ones. And I told him I can't. I don't have the POA's.

Son: When dad got back from out of state, just before Thanksgiving 2015, I started going over to see dad every day and have been doing it ever since; up to the writing this book on dad's life. By January 2016, he had care twenty-four hours seven days a week, at a clip of $480.00 per day or $14,400.00 per month. Dad's mentality got wore down in having the them in his house 24/7. He got so that he was using the F word, which dad never used around me and the people his entire life. One day, one of care givers left their diary of events on dad, while watching him, on dad's kitchen table. Revelational. Their persistence in ratcheting up the tension was building a case as to why dad needed constant care. The conflicts between my dad and care giver were occurring daily. Dad was changing locks to keep them out. Trashing the safe, they put his meds in. His staying up in fear something was going to happen to his house or him was starting to wear on dad.

Son: Stepping back a tad, that Christmas 2015 I was praying to God, with the tone; this man has done nothing but good to people. He has loved his wife and his sons unconditionally. He has given them; his life, his time and his resources without thinking twice and now some of these people were turning against him. God are You going to leave dad to die this way? This is Bullshit. As You have brought him out of these messes before, so will You now and I will witness it first hand versus dad telling me another story on how God had delivered him. It will be by my own mouth of how You delivered dad from this mess; and set him on a high place full of resources, that You give him once again to take him through the next season of his life.

Son: The twenty-four-hour care giver really messed dad up. I felt helpless mediating with limitations. I raised my three children by myself for 15+ yrs, without financial assistance from their mother and supervised union and non-union employees for over 30 yrs, so we had some experience with working with limitations and dead lines; that most people don't get to experience. A few weeks of dad being consistently restless with getting very little sleep in his own home; dad wanted to be put in the assistant living home; just to get away from it all. I said wait, if... details omitted... were gone, you would want to stay in your own home? He said yes. I asked some of the... details omitted... opinions on if they think dad needs 24hr care. They said he doesn't need twenty-four-hour care. Even the... details omitted... that interviewed dad to see if he needed assistant living, said dad didn't need twenty-four-hour care. But if he wanted to live at their facility, they would be glad to have him. The... details omitted... sent a thousand dollar down payment anyways.

Son: It's 02-04-16 and we're at the...details omitted... office. We asked them what's going on. Dad and I are in the dark, I'm mediating most of the time, no one knows who's in charge. So, the... details omitted... said how about if I give you control; would that help? I said that would be great. He said do you have five more minutes; we'll get it to you right now. I said, perfect. We walked out of the... details omitted... office spell bounded on what just happened. Can it be that God has truly intervened on my Dad's part again and I saw it with my very own eyes? Damn straight. Frkn A. There is a God who watches over my dad and I was looking at my dad's face with the look of breath of fresh air on it. OMG! How awesome is this people? Ok. Chill out. We're not out of the woods yet. Slow down so we can smooth this shit out.

Son: We preceded one step at a time. Not to rock the boat or draw attention to appearing to be self-driven. Keep reading it get's better.

Son: We first shut down financial access to dad's accounts. The... details omitted... was pissed. Details omitted... the paperwork that he had us sign voided out all previous authority. Details omitted... But it was signed sealed and delivered. I wasn't going to double check the... details omitted. Then we gave the authority to the bank, sent one to dad's Retirement Account Company and... details omitted.

Son: Next step shut down the... details omitted... We asked... details omitted, "was this a requirement or a recommendation?" Details omitted... "So, you're saying this was only a recommendation?" They said yes and it was based on the... details omitted... to have state it. I said thank you. We need to stop the... details omitted... or my dad will be out of cash in three months. We paid the bill and stopped going.

Son: We cut the... details omitted... down to a few days a week; then to a trail period of not at all. Details omitted... Now I'm feeling good about this sobering decision. I told them, now it's up to dad to prove he doesn't need twenty-four-hour care. A few weeks later, of dad getting longer hours of sleep, he's not as grumpy, getting back to his own self at cleaning himself and home up, making his own meals, etc.

Son: As of writing this book on dad's life in April 2017, dad has gone from since then to now without 24 in home care; almost fourteen months now. Thank you, God and Great Job Dad!

Son: Ok back what happened next? We were now in the market for a new doctor and a new attorney based on... details omitted.

Son: A few weeks later we believe dad's favor with God started to kick in. Dad's bother's daughter crossed our paths and gave us her dad's doctor's name. She stated that their doctor is so good that a state wide known hospital was trying to buy him out, to have on him on their team. But He said no. He is a doctor for the people and not for the corporation. It makes tons of sense now why health care is sky high expensive. It's being driven by corporate greed. Selling people hope through their outrageous drug prices. Ok. I'll stop banging. After a month and half, he accepted dad as a new patient, based on the doctor was doctoring his brother for over 25yrs. He checked dad out and said he was a normal 84 yr old man that has been out of the work force for 20+ years. Yaaay!! This is so cool, a doctor who is on dad's side and in dad's best interest. We had to go three times over the summer of 2016; hair follicle infection, a swollen elbow from a fall cleaning the yard up and deep chest congestion. All three times the prescriptions that his new doctor gave dad healed him within one week each. Awesome! And better yet, the doctor said he doesn't plan on scheduling any unnecessary visits. He'll trust dad, if something comes up and dad wants to see him, dad will come in because he actually needs medical help.

Son: Next dad wanted his cabin in his name only, so that he can have the peace that it will be split 50 50, when he passes on. So, we call the … details omitted… up in the June of 2016. The… details omitted… call it good with $10,000.00 and will sign the cabin back over to dad.

Son: Details omitted… this would be in the best interest of your dad. So, we located a title company in the County dad's cabin is in.

Son: The title company found no liens on the title. It was clean and it gave us the ok to move forward, per advice from dad's new attorney.

Son: We took out a home equity loan versus withdrawing another $10,000.00 from his retirement account which then dad would have to pay additional fed taxes on it, because he would go over again. Details omitted… The new attorney was buried back work logs and a family member in the hospital for a couple of weeks. The new attorney apologized and sent the proper paperwork to the… details omitted.

Son: About a month and a half elapsed and no word from the new attorney and… details omitted; that the proper paperwork was sent or received. So we emailed… details omitted… they claim they sent it. Called the new attorney, they said they didn't receive it. I told the new attorney to resent it again under registered mail, so that… details omitted… will have to sign off that they received it. I asked… details omitted… to send it registered mail as well, so that we can track it, if necessary. Maybe it got lost in the mail. Who knows? Hmm. God does. But it doesn't matter now.

Son: Recap. To date my dad has been restored off all of his assets. Yaaay!!! Dad sleeps all night without a break in sleep. He threw his old stove out of his house and we got a new stove. The store rep that sold us the new stove said he had served in Korea on the 38th parallel DMZ and it's still untouched. Dad is an awesome decorator. I have to admit he decorates better than mom did; and I honestly thought mom was good. He loved her so much; he loved how she decorated even though he knew he could do better.

Son: Dad occasionally has a bad day, but we figured out that it's in association of him eating a lot of sugar; strawberry short cake loaded with whip cream and ice cream, pecan pies, cookies. So, we've cut back and seen a difference.

Son: In the early part of April 2017, I noticed first thing while stepping through the kitchen doorway, dad had taken the TV off the fireplace wall and leaned it against the kitchen table. I looked at the fireplace wall and he had taken off the TV hardware as well. He said he wanted a new TV. So, we go to the store and he picks out the coolest curve smart TV there was. It was so smart it took me a few days to learn how to run it. He's back to watching TV again.

Son: I do know that I have lived to see how my dad's God has delivered him once again. And with that, I now can say, I was there and witnessed it with my own eyes. To me this is priceless; being able to tell my children, my grand children and my decedents of God delivered my dad through out his whole life. We will have the sales from the Ten Commandments My Father Taught Me, the Ten Commandments My Mother Taught Me, Can My Life Change, the New Friendship Bible, the Law of Unconditional Love and few other titles I hope to get published someday. These will be all blessings from my father; that a child can't get in a will and or a trust. Even if there are no sales with any of these books, it has done my spirit, soul and flesh good having this experience with dad.

Son: So, for a recap with what happen to these five that intentionally and or unintentionally were about to make dad's mourning time; the losing of the love of his life, into a living Hell. Even after weighing what was all said in this book on dad's life, these five might of honestly think they were right in doing what they did. Regardless this is where these five are right now. We hope... details omitted... is having a blast in heaven. Details omitted... who worked with the... details omitted... has been replaced by a new... details omitted...who cares for dad as a person; not a profit center; Details omitted... sent us a letter admitting that they had paperwork on file; that was only in the... details omitted and was told to submit the paperwork to the county, when dad was officially put into an assistant living facility. Details omitted also stated that they have shredded the document as we requested. And the... details omitted is no longer is employed by dad.

Son: Now with that back drop and without further due this is what my dad said to me on this last Valentine's Day 02-14-17.

Dad: I can live a life by myself, because I know about the double life. You can get use to living alone. I've made up my mind I'm going to stay single. I do not want to marry. I do not want to mess up what I had with my wife. In my mind we are still married. I want to go to Korea and see the 38th parallel again to see what it's like today.

Son: Wow dad, I've never heard you speak this statement so clear; about mom, now and moving forward. I'll go to Korea with you, if the money comes in from the sale of this book; then that will be a green light to go.

Dad: You would? Ok. If we don't go, it's ok too.

Son: Now how about playing a game of pool?

Son: Ever since I started seeing dad that December 2015 until now, we must play two to four games of pool every day. I'm thinking times by about 490 days that would equal

980 to 1960 games of pool. We're good, we still surprise ourselves how good and then we're down right horrible. I love seeing dad smile every day. And yes, he's still spitting out the witty words of wisdom. He is truly sent by God for this time and age to be an inspiration to us all. The way things keep going that might be another book someday. We had to stop at 103 Hell and Back Survival Tips just so that we could get his life story to the publisher.

Son: Dad and dad's life is truly the Ninth Wonder of the World.

And for what is worth mom, dad mentioned on 03-12-17 that you are still the inspiration that keeps him going. All is forgiven and he takes the blame for not setting up two wills; one for her and one for him.

☦ Publishing My Life Story ☦

D ad: I can't put words together, poor English person. i feel pretty good.

Son: When people read your book what do you hope people will get out of it?

Dad: Hope its easy reading.

Son: I'll try my best; while keeping it raw like if the person who is reading this was here with us listening and writing it down them self.

Son: Why did you choose "Hell and Back" as the title of your book?

Dad: It didn't come easy. When I went to Korea it was hell. I spent a lot of time outside. Fox holes; all kinds of weather. Even in the winter time, we had to be in the g-d damn fox holes. One of these days, they might get back together and be one Korea.

Son: While writing dad's memoirs down into this book, when I was about fifty-five percent done; I laid this book's journal on his car's roof. His glasses came up missing, so we spent about forty-five minutes in the house trying to find them. No luck. Then I notice he must of went out to the mailbox that day; his foot prints were in the snow, it was the later part of January 2017. Followed his foot prints on the snowy asphalt; going out to the mailbox by the two-lane highway. Nope. Nothing. Double checked on my way back. Nothing again. Seen a softball size chunk of asphalt out in the center of his circle drive. Picked up some loose plastic. Tossed the asphalt stone on a pile of stones around his circle driveway light pole and the loose plastic into the back end of his 1984 Chevy Truck; parked to be restored some day. Hopped into the car and off to the local restaurant we went; to do some more asking questions and writing more about dad's life story.

Son: You guessed it right. I realized I forgot to take this Hell and Back journal off the roof of his car. Holy shit, I said. My heart sunk into my stomach, along with all the associated thoughts that were flooding my brains. It fell off the roof onto the busy highway and got trashed like no other. I calmly drove knowing all would be lost and I would have to start all over again. Noooo. It was like leaving my child behind. Well sort of. It wasn't human but it was to me and I had to save it from dying a horrible death. The closer I got to dad's house; I saw what seemed like a book with white pages flopping back in forth in the light snowy breeze. Noooo. It's it. It's gots to be. I pulled off on the shoulder of the road, ran out into the middle of the two lanes. Stupid but desperate. My child was dying. And on coming car was really coming at me. I thought try grabbing it anyways. Miss. Damn. Got to grab anything and run like hell. As I grabbed anything and went to turn around, the on coming traffic was coming at me, I ran thinking this was stupidest thing I ever decided to do and I'm going to die. Made it to the car. My panic paralyzes me as I clung onto the driver's door on the outside, like a flat pancake. The on coming car honked its horn, like wow you're that stupid. But they had no idea what I was grabbing. Well maybe some day, if they read this book.

Son: Summary. This journal of dad's memoirs used to write his book, had gone to hell itself and came back. Too wild. Too freakn crazy. The journal looked as though it was starting to get the crap kicked out of it.

Son: I went inside dad's house with him, started to ask him questions about his life at the rental and colonial homes. He had fallen to sleep. So I decided to write this part of the book, while it was fearfully still in my mind.

Son: God was good. He put it all together. We were very fortunate to have all those good times and memories year after year; decade after decade. Most families have hard times; they hope, they plan and they try, but life eventually swallows them up. It's time that all mankind enjoys the family life like we did.

Dad: God is still good.

Son: I thought you were sleeping.

Dad: Smiles.

Son: Dad and I took a tour in the Fall of 2016 to see the update status of all the homes, he built over the years. His first big ranch home is still there and was looking good. When we stop along side of road; a lady that was apart of the family that lived there, came out in the yard towards dad's car. We introduced ourselves and let her know we are writing a book on dad's life; he and mom were the ones who built this house. She was surprised and was curious in wanting to know if there was ever a basement under the home, dad told her no. We thanked her and moved onto his next home.

Son: The next home he built was next to the one we just looked at. So as our eyes were looking to the west of his first home, we saw a bare lot. Nothing. I heard of a possible fire in one of the upstairs rooms but didn't know that it was torn down. The crazy part is that's how it started out; a bare lot adjacent west of his first home and now again it's a bare lot adjacent west of his first home. Drive by slow, stop and take a photo for the scrap book. Turn right and head down to the next corner, where he built his small ranch home. Cool. It's still there. It looks like they added on a half storage garage, cluttered but still being lived in. Yup; another photo. Ok now out of the subdivision and down to the farm.

Son: Wow. What a view. Definitely not what she used to be. All those big trees have been cut down except a few dead ones. A huge pond out back; not what I envisioned in my teens but I did see a pond in about the same area. The chicken coop is gone but a semi-buried foundation. Gated added driveway down about 100 feet, to give it more of privacy feel to it. The old east side property border fence line has been cleaned up; so, nothing divides it from the neighboring farmer.

Son: Dad had lost his new prescription glasses about the middle of Jan 2017. We looked all through his house. Nothing. There was about 2 to 4 inches of snow on the ground and driveway. Before we were going to go to the diner to write more on his Hell and Back Survival Tips, I thought I'm going to walk his circle driveway to his mailbox. His foot prints were there. As I get closer to the mailbox; I see stumbling foot steps around the mailbox, into the ditch to the telephone pole, across the driveway and into the ditch again. Damn dad had a bad day today and he didn't say anything about it. No glasses though. I get into his car and asked him if he had a bad day at the mailbox. He said yes; he fell.

Son: Fast forward to today, Feb 8th 2017; the snow all had melted away for the most part, with highlights of icy snow splattered randomly. As we both took his garbage out to the road, I got this urge to look for his glasses out by the mailbox area. So we both head to the mailbox. Found nothing; down into the ditch, nothing again. I picked up some winter trash in the ditch, then to the telephone pole. Bingo. Embedded into the icy grass; as I go to pick them up, I noticed some mud frozen on the lenses. This is freakn awesome. We found them. Now even his recently new bought prescription glasses had gone to hell and back. Goose bumps on how all these pieces are coming together for dad. I am truly witnessing God restoring dad yet again; perhaps to prepare him for the next season of his life.

Son: Thank you God for answering my prayers two Christmas's ago. My hands were tied, dad was being bull dozed into an assistant living place real fast. It was hard for me to believe that after all dad's been through and survived; that he was going be looking at four walls, his homes sold from underneath him and all alone. Locked away from his family, who he loved and gave his life; all his life. I asked God to please give me the chance to experience, personally with dad, like you did for dad from his foes over all of his life versus just hearing the stories of how you did. I can now personally say how God did it because I personally witnesses how God helped him get his assets back. This book is the witness proof of just that.

Son: This is a new update with this manuscript. This manuscript is not the original manuscript submitted to the publisher. The publisher rejected the first manuscript based on the real names and places documented within dad's life story manuscript. They explained it's the legal technical requirements in the industry of publishing. At first, it felt like the industry was trying to make us water down the truth, but with deeper thought on their technical jargon. I realized, regardless of us wanting to recognize and honor these people in dad's life story, if dad's life story rockets to the world class status lime light, these people might not want to be famous. These people have the right to privacy.

It makes sense when we look at that way. Also thinking, with world class famous status come those reporters who like to harass the locals for more information. Their hopes are scoring on some cheap self-centered publicity; they can't create on their own. Yup you guessed it before I can even write it. Dad's life story manuscript has now been added to his list of things going to hell and back. And by re-editing it, it has come back from hell too.

Son: This is a second new update to this manuscript. This and the next two short paragraphs are not in the original manuscript that was submitted to the publisher; the first and second times. We were trying to do a generic version of the actual events; that took place after dad's wife passed on, but the publisher is refusing to publish. Sorry people we are at their mercy. Many sorries to all those who are reading this book and would like to know; how another Korean Vet who loved his wife unconditionally all his life, was taken advantage of and the system wants to hide it.

Dad: Don't worry about it son; we tried. Leave it out. Maybe we can get it in a movie, documentary.

Son: Ok dad. This is not right though. When is the system going to defend the innocent?

Son: These above added events were added to document, how God has and will deliver him again from those as well.

Son: I've dedicated two to four hours everyday to be with dad, since December of 2015; to keep his freedoms as much as possible. I've spent countless of hours with him getting to know dad in a deeper way to capture his life story in book form; with the hope of inspiring others to not give up on their lives, their relationships and their legacies.

✝ My Family Photos ✝

The names of my siblings were omitted out of respect for their rights to privacy.

Me at third from the left with My 7 Siblings;
My Older Sister on the Left,
My Twin Sister second from the Left and My Oldest Brother
was in the house, at the time of this photo.

My Mother, Twin Sister and Me.

Me & My Sweet Heart Taking a Caribbean
Cruise in Our Elder Years

Me Reflecting on Life after My Wife's passing of
Little More than a Year and a Half, Afterwards.

✝ My Two Wars ✝

My War with Korea:

D ad: I was drafted. I wouldn't volunteer for any war. Nothing good comes out of war.

Son: What you learn about yourself?

Dad: I learned to be safe. **It brought out the skills that I already had.**

Son: What did you acquire from your War with Korea experience?

Dad: **It made it easier in helping me understand marriage better.**

My War with My Wife:

Dad: I volunteered to pursue My Free Movie Sweet Heart, the first time I saw her butt wiggle.

Son: Why did you choose to love your wife unconditionally all those years?

Dad: **I didn't realize how much I loved my wife until I learned how to love her 100% unconditionally. L. O. V. E. Period.**

Son: Wait a minute Dad, this blows the brains right out of my skull. This supersedes the generations, out lives all the ages. This was in the beginning, now and forever more.

Son: In another words; when I learn how to love someone unconditionally, I will then realize how much I love them.

Son: Or, I'm never going to know how much I love that person until I make the commitment of wanting to learn how to love that person 100% unconditionally twenty-four seven.

Son: We've got; wanting to be with someone all wrong. In general, we as a people think basically three reason of wanting to be with a specific potential companion:

1. Oh, this person is beautiful/sexy based on hormonal drives; and we do this and don't like that, a list of compatible characteristics.

2. Companionship is based on convenience. We've been living together for "x" years, we've had a child and or children; so we might as well get married. A backwards safe approach.

3. If we can be best friends at everything we do. That way after the intimate moments fade away, we still will want to be with each other because we've been there for each other; through the ups and downs of all the seasons of life together.

Son: All three of approaches are based on personal opinions that take a ton of faith and still have no guarantee of working; after "x" years of trying. They will all be short lived; because each one, the individuals still does not know how much they really do love each other. All these approaches plus whatever modifications, hybrids of and or something newly created out of the lab; will not/does not go to the core of what keeps companions together.

Son: Even Christianity is guilty of with, "husband love your wives as Christ loved the church," still doesn't cover it. Because with Christ dying; now he isn't physically here to help his bride/church go through her darker moments. Dying is the easy way out. It's living for that individual is harder. So, I died taking a bullet for my companion, what about all the other bullets that may come at my companion, after I'm dead? Wouldn't it be better, if I took out the source of who's shooting the bullets, so that we both can enjoy a long life together?

Son: All of the scriptures that motivate me by faith, to love that person are still done blindly, with no guarantees. Hit and miss. Marriage counseling is only one sided, if both are not bought into it and or short lived, when a new more complexed hardship consumes the couple. The marriage retreats/forwards are an awesome open forum to learn how to openly talk to each other, about how each other is wounding issues; but again, only good enough based on the effort of both people.

Son: What dad just said and how I explained it in further details; is the nucleus of any relationship. It's the nebula of any relationship. It clearly identifies for the person in question, how much love they have for another person and or how much that other person really loves them. By personally pursuing this, I will get/know the actual depth of my love for someone.

Son: Example: If I commit for ten years to learn how to love someone 100% unconditionally then four years into it, I get frustrated with that person and decide to stop wanting to learning how to love them, then I know for sure I only love that person 40%.

Son: This revelation supersedes all these thoughts, concepts and yes scripture references from any book of faith. Think about it. Let this absorb into our spirits, souls, minds and bodies.

Son: Real Unconditional Love is pure action with no words. The purest unconditional love contains no words. It's Word Free. It's Word Less. No lists of conditions are required, to do acts of real unconditional love.

Son: Fake (Self-Centered) Unconditional love is all words with no actions. The purest fake (Self-Centered) unconditional love contains no action. It's Action Free. It's Action Less. Lists of conditions are required before doing acts of fake (self-centered) unconditional love.

Son: This above time and creation revelation is a tangible tool that can be used to gauge how much I really love someone, and or if that person I'm committed to learning how to love, is committed to learning how to love me.

Son: For the complete revelation that was birthed from dads "I didn't realize how much I loved my wife until I learned how to love her 100% unconditionally" statement; read the book *The Law of Unconditional Love*. Author Optimum Vizhan; Published by Trafford Publishing.

✝ Summary of Accomplishments ✝

1. Built 4 New Homes.
2. 39.5 yrs as Utility Company Employee; took $200,000.00+ buy out.
3. Built 1 New Cabin Mostly out of Cedar Telephone Poles.
4. Built 1 New Very Small Cabin.
5. Own 80 Acre Farm: Farmed it, completely remodeled farm house and developed property.
6. Secretary of the Local Veteran of Foreign Wars.
7. Mason.
8. Florida Trips 30 + yrs.
9. Bought and restored a trailer in a Ft Meyers FL.
10. 3 Trips out West. One along Southern States to Arizona and two along Northern States to Yellowstone Wyoming.
11. Had 2 boys, 4 Grand Children and 7 Great Grand Children.
12. Owed 3 dogs, 2 Roasters, 3 Hens, 3 Rabbits, 2 Horses, 30 Cats.
13. Served in Korean War 1 yr and 9 months; as a Private then Corporal.
14. Drove General around in Jeep in Korean War.
15. Fell off the Roof of Single-Story home. No injuries got back up on roof to finish roofing it same day.
16. Fell off second story scaffolding with no injuries.

17. Water Skied in Summers and did some Solemn Skiing.
18. Went to the 8ᵗʰ Grade in School.
19. Got GED when transferred to the Gas Department the Utility Company worked for.
20. Had 21ˢᵗ Birthday on the 38ᵗʰ Parallel, during 1ˢᵗ Korean War.
21. Twin to his twin sister.
22. Survived a two-truck head on collision with only crushed ribs and six weeks off of work.
23. Survived a Ram Head Butt at 3 years old into the Family's Steel Wheel Tractor with "V" shapes welded on them for traction.
24. Work about 7 months for auto manufacturing company's; long enough to earn union card.
25. Learned how to write Hebrew.
26. Learned how to fly a single engine airplane.
27. Sit for 2 yrs straight on Saturdays and Wednesdays in a Local Jewish Synagogue.
28. Indian Guides Father participant.
29. Taught 4h boys how to wire a light bulb from scratch, in a 3-week period.
30. Went to Alaska 3 times. 1 Alaska cruise. 2 times with my wife.
31. Took 2 Caribbean Cruises.
32. Travel to Virginia Beach Virginia to tour CBN then up the East Coast.
33. Owned and Ran Flower Shop, called Dick Florist.
34. Raised Gladiolas from the banks of the Creek that ran through the father's farm and sold in the market places of Lennon, Miller Rd and Ballenger and the Flint Farmers Market.
35. Successful Stock Investor.
36. Married for 62 yrs to his wife.
37. Knew his wife since she was 13yrs old, for a total of 67 yrs.

38. Skated with one foot each with his twin sister on the family farm pond.
39. Trimmed and Cut Trees for the wealthy home owners living in Flint Michigan.
40. Milked 2 cows 8 tits each, 2 times a day for 10 years by hand. (Dad says, it seemed like forever).

✝ My Hell n Back Survival Tips™ ✝

S on: One of the rewarding opportunities in helping dad write his life story in book form; was asking him what nuggets of wisdom/thoughts he had, that got him through and as well obtained from; while going through his Hell and Back experiences. It was like God giving me a second chance in life, to connect with my father as a son. After a few diner strawberry short cakes and Flint Coney dogs', Dad came up with a 103 Hell and Back Survival Tips for us to consider, when going through the different seasons of our lives.

1. **Have No Thoughts of Dying.** Understand living. I think God figures it out pretty even. He gives us a chance to live a full life. Some people like to rush it; by getting sick, drive to fast. My dad was 96 when he pasted.
2. **RRRRRRRRRRRRRRR.** Get Focused. Look Out. Rrrrrrrrrrrrrrr.
3. **Stay Out of Trouble. Be Smart.** I use to get into a lot of trouble. My trouble making friend lived a few miles down the road from my dad's farm. Wrestle a lot. No boxing, wrestle.
4. **Pick Good Friends.** It's Easier When You Have a Good Mother and Father. They want somebody to be with. If two different personalities; won't stay together very long.

5. **Stay Single.** Never get the idea of chasing women or men or getting married. Some get married right away without being single first. So that if I'm single one day, I'll be at peace with it.
6. **God's the Boss.** Man can't do what the hell He wants. God gets man to do His work; but if doesn't, He can.
7. **When We're Married, We have Several Bosses.** Most women like to boss. Man thinks he's the boss but he's fooling himself.
8. **Stay Away from Booze.** Always had around house. Dad had hard cider around from the apple cider mill. We would have several barrels of cider and hard cider. Dad would always let several; seven to nine, drunks hang around. Dad would give it away. Dad would not charge them. They would hang out half the night. Mom would have one of my brothers get hard cider up from cellar, drag up steps and roll up steps. Throw out, drain out of barrels onto ground. Good sign to drunks that all done. They went back to the bars. They would get so drunk they would piss their pants; because you can get hooked on it.
9. **Eat a Lot of Ice Cream.** One of my brothers and I would make ice-cream when rest the family went to town. Easy to make. Eight quarts of ice-cream. Jersey cow eighty percent cream. We had that one cow just for ice-cream. Just a desert.
10. **Play Hard, Work Hard and Sleep Hard.** Good to play hard. When we were kids, we played hard. Keeps the old blood circulating to get into low spots. Gives you good rest. Keeps your body up and kicking. If haven't learned by sixteen just horsing around then.
11. **Laugh a Lot.** Makes yah smart. Gives yah something to think about. Son: You have to be smart to be funny.

12. **Everyone Should Know How to Milk a Cow.** To see where the milk comes from. Some kids like to learn; some don't. Secret to milking a cow; be gentle. Don't pinch them or they'll swatch you with their tail on back of head. Every morning they will be filled up with milk. Twice as big as my hand. We had twenty-four cows. Milk a cow in fifteen minutes. Milk all tits. Use both hands. Gently squeeze until done. Then do stripping. Two fingers thumb and index; get another two cups. If didn't strip them they would dry up. All of us milking cows before school and before supper. Feed them too. Like to eat hay and grain. Carried water to them. Modern farms had water faucets bowl about gallon water. We milked cows, feed, let go out to pasture graze around. Planted clover. Hard summer; dry up hay, still eat it. Seems to even out. No problem. Feeding hay, clover and alfalfa. Stalls in, hook them in brace. Stations for each cow to hold them.

13. **Always Have Time to Stop and Smell the Roses.** It's just a saying. You get out of it whatever you want out of it. Don't really have to stop, just keep on a smelling.

14. **Every Kid Should Grow Up on a Farm.** Every kid doesn't need to grow up on farm. Go where he wants to go. Do everything on the farm. Sets you up to go where ever you want to go. A lot of different jobs on a farm.

15. **I did what I wanted to do as a Teenager.** Hopefully they'll find something they like to do. Most change several times before they find something. I didn't like farming, so I left home and restored a green house for one year rent free. Got ready for business. Hired heavy set guy five feet five inches. One hundred eighty-two hundred pounds. Chewed tobacco. He could spit. I told him to quick spitting there are women around here. Eighteen to nineteen people working for me. Guy was from neighboring

town. Good worker. Nobody took green house over when I left. Sold flowers at farmers market, Seymour road. Green house gives you a break in winter. Good summer job.

16. **When Making decisions and others think your nuts take it like a man and do it anyways.** It will just work out. They don't know what their talking about.

17. **Got to hang on the Tiger's Tail.** Cuz I know he can pull you around and get you out of trouble.

18. **Being Last Born gives you the perspective of go with the flow.** First thing you know, kindergarten playing, before you know your in-grade school. Get big picture upfront. Not worrying about big picture, enjoy big picture.

19. **Raise Hell. – So Hell Knows You are in Charge.** Get a little excitement. Change your normal routine. The surroundings you're in helps get you through your teenage years. A lot of company. There's a place for everything. A time. Son: In another words kick hell in the Ass so hard that Hell will want you to leave. Do an extreme make over first, so that you leave your mark and they'll remember who was there long after you leave.

20. **Slow Down and Think What You're Doing.** Not enough in one thing to keep you busy all the time. Slow down. Grow older. Pace paces. Slow paces. Grows and goes through stages it seems to go good. Balances out.

21. **Think to Do Good.** If you raise hell it's going to slow you down in your activities. Very easy to get into trouble.

22. **Do Something Good.** Helps them stay out of trouble, stay out of jail.

23. **Go Where You Have to Go and Take it Slow and Easy.** If you rush into stuff you usually get into trouble, make a mistake.

24. **Enjoy Today.** Best thing to do. Go to fast you get into trouble. Least you'll be out of troubles.

25. **Play A Lot.** Its more fun. Stop once and awhile and get your work done.

26. **Be More Careful.** Listen to learn yourself to know when to be careful.

27. **It's Ok to be Embarrassed When We Fall Down.** Can't help it. If able get right back up.

28. **We Don't Know What We're Saying until We can Say it Backwards.**

29. **It would be nice if We Could put Every thing in a Bag, Shake it up and whatever falls out; do it.**

30. **I'm going to Stick in there, so that I can say I stuck it out.**

31. **Get Good Rest so We can Have a Good Day.** Get all drained out if don't.

32. **If You're Young Have More Children.** Makes a healthy family; to me it does. All together, some help one another. Older ones will carry the smaller ones on their backs. Bigger families are better.

33. **We can be Stupid at Any Age.** Don't have to know everything.

34. **Let Your Companion Say What They Need to Say and Just Listen.** So won't make the same mistake.

35. **If Your Spouse Wants to Leave Let them.** You'll find out How Much They Really Love You.

36. **Give Your Spouse Room to let them do What They want to do.** Don't want to tie them down all the time. So they can be themselves.

37. **Keep One Tire in Plow Furrow and Your Eyes on a Fence Post a Half Mile Out and You'll Plow a Straight Line.**

38. **The Best Time to Milk a Cow is between 4am and 6am and then again between 4pm and 6pm.** If you don't milk them at the same time they'll dry up. If not regular time they'll stop giving milk. Have to be consistent. Can't change a cow's milking time. If don't line up with it, she won't give any milk.

39. **Start Your Day Working and Finish Your Day Working.** Gets the blood flowing. Paces yourself. Somedays might not have anything to do; that's when you can take a vacation. Brings things up to speed.

40. **Learn How to Play Hard.** Gets all the benefits of moving the body.

41. **Learn How to Have a Family.** Getting the chance of knowing the purpose of being the head of family. See how the children work together.

42. **Learn How to Raise a Family.** Might be for more than one reason. Might not want a big family.

43. **Do it until it Becomes Automatically Naturally.** Do what you want to do. Changing times of milking a cow, the cow will dry up sooner than later.

44. **Have Fun Working Hard.** It lets us enjoy it better. Time goes by faster.

45. **Have Fun Having a Family.** Enjoy it more.

46. **Have Fun Raising a Family.** Enjoy it more.

47. **Do it until it Becomes Automatically Naturally so that You can Enjoy it.**

48. **Take Your Spouse in Your Arms and Hold Them.** Shows them that you love them. Naturally do it. Don't ask. Do naturally.

49. **Don't Look at Handicaps as Handicaps. It's something you do naturally with your spouse.** Take it as it comes. If can fix, ok. If not, thank God for it.

50. **Choose Jobs Based on Your Likes so that You will like your job.** I liked freedom so I picked and outside job.

51. **Never to Old to be a Kid.** I think a kid has the knowledge and ambition to do what they do. We all have to go through that kid stage.

52. **Hold Your Stick up Straight.** It's possible.

53. **Focus 100% on the job you're working on.** Once you understand the job 100% then you'll have time to think of the next job or going forward easier.

54. **Never take anything serious.** Something doesn't go normal or planned; think it over to keep it going. Sometimes you put stuff in that doesn't do a damn thing for what you're trying to do. Sometimes you can back off and let it work out.

55. **Have No Regrets.** I have no regrets. If something doesn't work out, then that's what was supposed to happen. Try two to three times and doesn't work out then that's what was to be. Best thing to do is keep on mind and you can always go back to it or accept that's the best it gets.

56. **If I had to do it all Over Again I would do it.** Cuz you could add in or out, if want to do; to complete it.

57. **A lot of brothers and sisters means you'll have someone to play with and Keep Out of Mom's and Dad's Hair.** They might give you a hair cut.

58. **Don't Go to Far into Something Until you Learn it.**

59. **We will always have to Learn How to Milk a Cow and Plant a Field.**

60. **No Matter who Starts a Fight will get Tired Out and Stop.**

61. **It Pays to be a Good Cook for Oneself, Family and or to Sell.**

62. **If Your too Short Stand on a Piece of Paper.**

63. **Before You Get a Pet for Your Child be Willing to Take Care of it Yourself.** If not, it would be better to spend that time with your child. You're with them the shortest amount of time.

64. **Play with Your Grand Children.**

65. **Holidays Make Good Breaks.**

66. **Family Vacations are the Best.** It seems like it is.

67. **Always Have Time for Your Favorite Recreation.**

68. **When Someone Makes Fun of You and You Don't Like It, You Take It. Let Them Think It Doesn't Bother You.**

69. **Have Good Humor.** It's good to have humor. Don't want to be serious all the time.

70. **Stay Away from Pranks.** That's not REAL fun; fake fun.

71. **There's Always a Kid Out There Who Wants to Race.**

72. **Slow is Better than Being Fast.** You can think better when you're slow.

73. **If You Find Yourself Alone Take Up Reading to Pass the Time by Easier.**

74. **Have at Least One Boy and One Girl Before Stop Having Children so that They can Relate to Each Other.**

75. **The More Children You Have the Easier it is to Raise Them.** The Oldest Helps Out.

76. **If I Wake Up in the Morning and Don't Have a Tag on My Toe Then I know it's Going to be a Good Day.**

77. **It's Good to Have Both Spouses Know How to Take Care of the Money so If One Can't the Other Can.**

78. **Find a Good Woman/Man.** Pretty hard. Study. Still might not find anybody. They got to be willing to help each other. It's a must to get along in the beginning. If do not want to communicate, it's not going to work. Going to be miserable for rest of life. If they don't want to listen then no hope of communicating. Sorry you're going to have to go; buy them a bus ticket. They know better.

79. **When going on dates make sure the other one is having fun and focus on them only.**

80. **Babies give us a sense of responsibility.** I wanted to do it coming from a big family.

81. **Wait to Have Kids After Been Married a Few Years.**

82. **Travel Before Having Kids; if You Like to Travel. Travel First. Get Traveling Done First.**

83. **When the wife tells you to whip the child, think it's a good idea.**

84. **Work Hard to Making the Family Bond Stronger.**

85. **Never too Old to be a Grand Parent.** To be a grand parent you re are going to be a little older. They look like grand parents. If you look like a grand parent mite as well be one.

86. **Each Season has Its Own Time.** Summer, Fall, Winter and Spring; we go through four seasons. Breaks up your year; variety. We do a little bit different in each one. If we had one season, we wouldn't like it. We would view life from that one season.

87. **Pack Light.** Don't have to worry about everything.

88. **We're the Greatest Miracle that God Created. – ref Og Mindo.**

89. **Give Everything to God because He's going to give you everything.** He's already done it. If we don't take it we lose it. If we take it and do right with it, it will be good to us. We should be smart enough to know. If not, they know something about it; even if it's a little bit. Grow up, go to school, buy things; God's furnishes all that, plus.

90. **Take Time to Enjoy the Season We are in – It Seems to Even Itself Out.** No Season was fast.

91. **Thank Your Loved Ones for Hanging in There and around;** if They Didn't we wouldn't be Where We are Today.

92. **Being Spoiled Straightens Us Out.** It Ends Up Helping Us Understand what's Really Important.

93. **The Top Three Investments: Invest Into Something Easy, An Easy Hobby and Playing Sharper Pool.**

94. **If You Want to Travel be Smart about It** – Look Out for Yourself.

95. **Have Two Wills, One for Yourself and One for Your Spouse;** the Survivor Might Have Different Plans.

96. **Only Take the Advice From People Who Experienced What You Have Experienced.**

97. **Don't Spend Much on Weddings.** Just enough to get it done. The money is going to last long or short. When get married in younger years don't have a lot of money.
98. **Sports Keeps Your Body Healthy.**
99. **Learn How to Love with Your Actions; Have Fun Loving with Your Actions. Do it until it's automatically Natural so You Can Enjoy Loving with Your Actions.**
100. **The Best Advice a Father can Tell His Son is "Hang onto Your Money."**
101. **The Best Advice a Father can Tell His Daughter is "Stay Away from Drunks; They'll Ruin Your Life."**
102. **It's Very Important to Keep God in Mind All the Time Because That's Where it All Starts and Ends.**
103. **When Your Lover and or Child Passes before You, Keep Them Close to Your Heart so You will Keep Communicating with Them.** That Continual Fellowship will be Good Medicine for Your Life.

Son: This felt like to me what people say, this is an Opportunity of a Lifetime. Being able to hang out with Dad, in his own home and time and write down the wisdom he learned from his accumulated life experiences. He grew up on a farm that supported the community. Fell in love with his thirteen-year-old sweet heart and never left her side in the good times and bad times. He went to the eighth grade. Raised gladiolas from the rich farm creek banks then sold a dozen of them for seventy-five cents to guys getting out of work. Flower shop owner that employed twelve people. Drafted into the Korean War; Married, waited seven years to have kids. Had two boys, has seven great grandchildren, married 62 yrs. He knows how to build a home from the ground up inside and out, built four homes, and remodeled a farm house, built two cabins after working 40 hr weeks at his career job. On the edge of death vehicle accident, heart attack and bypass surgery. He cared for his diabetic wife for forty plus years. Travel out west three times and to Florida over 20 plus times. Where he bought a trailer home and lived there in the winter months for several years. He went on cruises. He joined the Masons, secretary of Veterans. He helped people build their cabins, repair their vehicles, volunteer for several non-profits. He learned how to fly a single engine air plane. He learned how to write Hebrew. He attended and observed Jewish synagogue Saturday and Wednesday services. He has been a widow for almost two years as of now. He did all this without rushing. It came natural to him to stay busy. He would never let you know he was in a rush, in pain and or having a bad day. I never saw dad having a bad day where it pissed him off and it affected everyone around him. He was never angry at people, life and or God. He was and is a master at going with the flow and being at peace with it. He wasn't rich to do all these things; he had to rejuggle his resources to make it happen. He's not a saint that should be canonized. He's just a normal man, who blends in at any local grocery and department store. He was never into bling bling; wearing clothes and accessories to get attention.

Son: **A pope** isn't a good example of a man. He lives a sheltered fantasy life isolated from the real life of the common man. **A successful international business man** is busy running his business and into showing off his wealth from being "successful." **A celebrity** lives in the confines of marketing their entertaining talents. And even though **Christ** is our Elder brother of an example on how to live life, He too is not a real-life example. Yes, He is perfect God in the flesh; it's an automatic given that He is going to be perfect at whatever He does. But He was never just a physical man; who became a physical husband and have physical children like the rest of mankind. Some writings suggested He did but regardless, He was consumed more with liberating mankind from their self-inflicted bondages; from the results of being self-centered versus having and unconditionally loving a family. All these examples are living in fancy land of what REAL life is. Not condemning any of these choices of life; but there just not common enough to be real life examples, on how to live life for the rest of the 99.99% population. **All four of these examples** can not come and go as they please without sticking out in the crowds of people. Their children will more than likely not be able to associate with the rest of the population; as they choose without being recognized as well.

Son: **My dad is the example** of what all men should aspire to be for themselves, their companions, their families and the communities they live it; no matter the age, religion, culture or time in history. He stands out in connecting with his loved ones around him, in every day life while at the same time compassionately fitting in with the crowds as a common man. He listens more than he talks. His actions are honorable, ethical and gentle. He only expresses his love in and with his actions. He is wise, humorous and driven. He worked hard, played hard and slept hard while being at peace with his environment; automatically, naturally to the point he enjoys it.

Son: Then to add to this feel of the conversation, I was married, divorced, single parent raising my three children by myself for 15+ years, supervisor for 30+ yrs over union and non-union employees working under the same roof, entrepreneur, build websites that get in the top ten online search engines, published author of the current five books this being the 6th title: Maximizing the Armor of God, His Life, New Friendship Bible, the President's Apocalypse, Can My Life Change, and now this Hell and Back, plus 70+ other titles in my head yet to write, grandfather of current seven children. So, with these two mindsets sitting down together and going through about the same synchronized seasons in both our lives; I asked dad what seemed a million questions about his life, to glean his/these 103 wise sayings.

Son: His hope is; others will be inspired to be the best they can be, at whatever they pursue, while sharing it 100%

with a companion and family naturally automatically; so that they all can enjoy it together, loving one another 100% unconditionally.

Son: Writing dad's life story for him is and was priceless. It was a way of repaying dad back; for all what he has done for me, throughout my life. I got to learn more about myself and how to be at peace with oneself.

Son: Every child should set down with their parents and ask them million+ questions about their lives and publish it in book form. The mindset of publishing my parent's life story; will cause me to thoroughly ask questions about my parents' life changing events versus random brief conversations about their life. This format of listening, writing and rereading their life story; will create a stronger bond between the child and the parent. This stronger bond will bring closure to the child and parents past, present and future relationship with each other. This closure will allow the child and the parent to grow their current relationship into a more enriching relationship.

Son: Dad did you ever think you would have a son who would ask you all these questions?

Dad: No.

Son: Didn't see it coming?

Dad: No. (Dad Chuckles).

Son: Thank you Dad! A lot of these Hell and Back Survival Tips made me; smile, think and want to try, especially if I get the opportunity to marry and have another family.

☦ How to Love Someone Unconditionally ☦

1. It's a Choice.
2. It Should be Easy.
3. If They Don't Love Who There Around, They're not Happy.
4. Think They're the Greatest Person in the World.
5. Look Out for Them.
6. Always Love Them.
7. Treat Your Wife Real Good, that's Your Only Hope of Survival.

✝ Dual Ending I ✝

S on: Current. At the time of this writing and publishing this book, Dad is working on trying to stay out of an Assistant Living Facility.

Son: I visit dad everyday for a few hours. We play pool, go out to eat four to five times a week, go to bank, groceries and clothing. We Shop when necessary. Very thankful I and my dad live close by or he would be living with me in my home or worse case in an Assistant Living Facility.

Son: Dad has pictures of his free movie sweet heart through out and in every room of the house. Dad still remembers the day he met her at the Free Movies. It still feels like it was just yesterday they met for the first time.

Son: Dad likes playing the sweep stakes and buying lottery tickets in hopes of winning. He says he's played enough all these years it's his turn to win.

Son: Dad is enjoying the peace and quiet of living in his own home. Dad says he's lived a full life. He's ready to go, if God's says its time.

Son: An Odd Lot of Questions, I would like to ask you Dad…

Son: What's Your Favorite Color?

Dad: Blue.

Son: What's the Coolest Thing About the 20th Century?

Dad: Every One Hundred Years Things Don't Change a Whole Hell of a Lot.

Son: How Could You Get Mom to Laugh?

Dad: I never took anything serious.

Son: What Makes a Man, A Real Man?

Dad: I don't know; a real man. There's no limit to being real. Keep doing good.

✝ Dual Ending II ✝

S on: If God Blesses dad with Extra Income; either through winning the lottery, the sales of this book and or from a movie on his life story then he would strongly consider buying part and or all of his father's homestead. It would make his life story an even greater life story, coming full circle. They say all good stories finish where they started and that would perhaps be dad's rightful ending. Looking in dad's father's eyes and telling him he would buy him out; wasn't an, I'm better than you statement. It was more of; dad I understand how you make this work and know how to perpetuate it; no matter what the season is in any century. I might leave to pursue what the 20th century has to offer, but I will return after I have had a wife and family, to pick up where you left off. I'm a Koan; just like you dad and I will continue the Koan Legacy. Until then, I'll let my brother's do what they see fit.

Son: Then develop into the businesses that his father perhaps would have made it into; if he were still alive today. Back in his day he would produce things that he could harvest every month, to take care of his family. Increased acreage ownership; all from his second-grade education. If I remember right, He ended up with approximately 200+ acres and over 200+ thousand dollars in cash when he passed on.

Son: To continue his dad's legacy, he would develop products that could be sold at local brand name grocery stores. Not to compete with his family but enhance the options that are not currently available.

Son: Dad is not much of a fighter, more of a hard-working entertainer who loves his family and sees great things for them and the world.

Son: If this doesn't happen, dad still has lived a full life and his hope for the generations to come is; couples all over the world will experience what its like to totally be in love with each other unconditionally. Even to the point of giving them your wallet, time, life, dignity and mind; with no judgment, intimidation or physical abuse.

Son: Dad is not a religious man either, but has read about how we are to love our spouse, as Christ did the church. I guess you could say dad's life was an example of that; naturally without being aware of the scripture reference for most of his life.

✝ Significant Dates ✝

RICHARD KOAN IS BORN
07-26-1932
As An Unplanned Twin

NORTH KOREA INVADES SOUTH KOREA
06-25-1950

RICHARD KOAN DRAFTED TO SERVE
in **KOREAN WAR** on
US ARMY 160TH INF REGT
SERVED ON FRONT LINE 2ND DIV
11-06-52

RICHARD and HIS SWEET HEART GET MARRIED
03-28-53

CEASE FIRE TRUCE SIGNED
07-27-53

The Day before is Richard Koan's 21st Birthday. Back in the Day this would be his official "I am an Adult Now" Birthday. So, Richard is "Enjoying" his birthday on 07-26 on the 38th parallel, knowing he is now an adult and the next day he would be going across the 38th parallel to his death. However, that night, at midnight of 07-27-53 a truce was declared. Richard did not have to cross over on 07-27-53. This was truly an awesome birthday gift from God; another moment of deliverance in Richard's life... What are the odds in someone in the Korean War having a birthday the day before the truce? Ok there might of; even on the day of the truce itself. But what are the odds of that man's birthday being born as a twin; not as twin brothers, but as sister and brother twins? This is cut in stone proof the dad has been set aside to be an inspiration; to all families, of all cultures, of all ages, for the 21st century and beyond.

This Truce would provide 1500 square miles of Territory for South Korea, protected by the two-mile-Wide Demilitarization Zone. As of 04-21-17 this DMZ still exists.

RICHARD KOAN DISCHARGED FROM SERVICE
RECEIVED 5 METALS:
08-21-54

NORTH KOREA INVADES SOUTH KOREA
2nd KOREAN WAR – UNPUBLICIZED.
11-02-66 to 12-03-69

92 Servicemen lost their lives and wasn't publically recognized for it until the 50th Anniversary 11-02-16, thanks to the Veterans of Foreign Wars.

RICHARD KOAN RETIRED FROM WORK LIFE
08-01-94

HIS WIFE WRITES HER MEMOIRS ON
08-08-08
Yup.

NORTH KOREA DECLARES 38TH PARALLEL
PEACE AGREEMENT INVALID
03-11-13

RICHARD'S SWEET HEART PASSES ON FROM THIS LIFE
07-07-15

RICHARD KOAN'S LIFE STORY IS COPYRIGHTED ON
03-28-17

PREDICTION: NORTH AND SOUTH KOREA
ARE REUNITED as KOREA
Around or After 06-25-2020

This would put an end to the war, threats of war and being on war alert that has tormented their people, their land and their nation for seventy years. This would be based on three events that have happened in prior history. East and West Germany reunited as one nation as old Germany on 10-03-1990. North and South Vietnam reunited as one nation as Socialist Republic of Vietnam on 07-02-1976. 606 BC Israel went into captivity under Babylon in for seventy years, and then released to return to their home land in 536BC.

Estimates of 165,000 service personnel have been rotated over the years in South Korea, but few did duty on the DMZ.

✝ Additional Books & Resources Related to Hell and Back ✝

The Law of Unconditional Lov

This is Book was birthed from my dad's two war experiences; one with Korea and the other with his wife. While he said no good comes from war; his Korean War experience made it easier for him to understand marriage better. And the War with His Wife experience; revealed to him, he didn't realize how much he loved his wife until he learned how to love her unconditionally, one hundred percent. This book expands this revelation into an actual gauge, that guarantees me to know how much I love someone and or how much someone loves me instantly. Author: Optimum Vizhan. Publisher: Trafford Publishing.

The Ten Commandments My Father Taught Me

This is Book goes into more depth of who the man, father and grandfather Richard Koan is, through my view being his son. He did not specifically teach His Ten Commandments to me, he was a man of few words and all action; be it gentle, firm or living life beside you. These Ten Commandments are a bullet point summary of how I categorized what dad taught me as a son; to help me go through my life, while dad was committed to my mother through the good and the bad times. It is and was a truly honor and privilege, in being Richard Koan's son. I am deeply indebted to God for putting us together as father and son, man and man, father and father, grand father and grandfather. Author: Optimum Vizhan. Publisher: Trafford Publishing.

My Fathers Favor

This is the Prayer I would pray through out the week for my father …. "The breath and the sound of Your Blood, Word, Love, Spirit and Seal; permeate, saturate and overflow with unprecedented favor in regenerating, renewing and restoring full strength, full life and full prosperity; on, in, with, through and around my fathers: spirit, soul, body, flesh, bones, bone marrow, blood, blood veins, blood heart, mind, eyes, senses, hand eye depth perception, eye hand clarity, daily mental clarity, memory system, accumulative mental clarity, memory trees, digestion system, nervous system, skin, hair, liver, kidneys, lungs, reproductive system, wisdom, peace, rest, entrepreneur skills creating successful products, with successful marketing, with successful sales, with successful manufacturing, with successful distribution, with successful employee profits; all for Your Glory and the restoration of dad's life and his legacy. The same for Israel, Jerusalem, USA, Ukraine, France, UK, Egypt, Russia, China, Koreas, India, Persia, Brazil, Mexico, Canada and the rest of the world, my employer, my home town. Now according to Act 16:31, Gal 6:7-8, Gen 12:3 and Psalm 122:6; I and my household receive the same thing." As I was getting to the end of writing and getting dad's life story published, I started to receive my father's favor. An old work friend called me up and wanted me to write his book for him; that he would split the profits 50/50. A couple of months later, I started taking a trading options training class. A few weeks into the class it was cancelled. They ended up putting me another options training class for one year FREE; at a savings of $2600.00. Could this be it? I receive my biological father's favor when I unconditionally help him further his success as an individual. When I do this unconditionally to the point of tangibly manifesting for him, then my heavenly father will bless me with new tangible resources that will effortlessly establish me in the midst of my hell. Sequel to this book is the *Maximizing the Armor of God manual and the pro series.* Author: Optimum Vizhan. Publisher: Trafford Publishing.

Maximizing the Armor of God manual

This is Book is a Revolutionary New Approach in handling death, divorce, depression, debt, addictions, fear, loneliness, physical limitations, self-centeredness and everything else that's destroying our lives! This is not another prayer book on confession, fasting and positive profession against evil. It's simple, brief and revelationally effective.

It's simple. The Word of God sets us free to enjoy life with no guilt. Religion convinces us our guilt is removed when we submit to her.

It's brief. The Word of God automatically transforms our lives when we let it. Religion keeps adding to our "to do list" to make sure we will always feel guilty.

It's revelationally effective. The Word of God brings unity. Religion brings judgment and isolation.

Maximizing the Armor of God, along with four other books; The Art of Spiritual Warfare, The Five Offices, New Revelations on Revelations and The Kings in Christ's Kingdom make up a five book series. This series allows us to take the logistics of the Armor of God, combined with harnessing our thoughts, to give us impenetrateable Spiritual Armor of God to the Nth Degree. Author: Optimum Vizhan. Publisher: Trafford Publishing.

The Ten Commandments My Mother Taught Me

This is Book goes into more depth of who the woman, mother and grandmother Sally Koan is, through my view of being her son. She did not specifically teach Her Ten Commandments to me, she was a woman of many words and little action; be it gentle, firm or living life beside you. These Ten Commandments are a bullet point summary of how I categorized what mom taught me as a son; to help me go through my life; while she committed to being with my father through the good and the bad times. It is and was a truly honor and privilege in being my mother's son. I am deeply indebted to God for putting us together as mother and son, woman and man, mother and father, grandmother and grandfather. Author: Optimum Vizhan. Publisher: Trafford Publishing.

The New Friendship Bible

The NFB is written in the theme of God desiring to have friends made in His likeness. His desire emerges from the back drop of basking in His omnipresence for countless of eons. Then at one moment, He finds Himself deep in His loneliness. After wrestling with Himself, for more eons, He realizes He longs for a friend. With every bit of His infinite wisdom, He sets out in pursuit to remove all of His loneliness. This adventure will take Him to all of the edges of His omni existence; in all of His infinite dimensions. He will make eternal commitments and personal sacrifices to reassure Himself, that our friendship with Him; will not be by force, not by intimidation and defiantly not by keeping a set of rules.

The NFB was created with new books and thoughts based on a compilation of traditionally accepted scriptures; for the purpose of encouraging us to pursue a more enriching relationship with God.

Over 400 Meditationals, for personal and or group studies, were added through out the NFB to stimulate our hearts, our minds to embrace God's friendship with us, in a fresh new way.

With the NFB, we can imagine God: desiring to have an unconditional love friendship with us versus through a list of rules; revealing His new friendship with those who have never seen or heard His story before; and His manifesting a deeper friendship with us, through our life's passions, through our particular needs and through our businesses. Author: Optimum Vizhan. Publisher: Trafford Publishing.

Can My Life Change

Can My Life Change compassionately identifies my justifiable "bad" routines and counters them with "good" routines *in over 365 Plus Routine Changing Inspirational* Routines are like double edged swords. One side of the blade helps me cut through my distractions, so I can obtain my goals. While the other side hypnotizes me into believing my deliverance comes from a routine. Ironically, the true end results of all routines make me complacent and further away from obtaining my desires.

The key to *Can My Life Change* is in mastering how I can break my routine self-induced trances. I start by clearing my mind with any of the 365 Plus Inspirationals. Then practice derailing any of my current routines that I'm addicted to. It could be doing an unplanned fast to break a feeding routine, eating a new food group to change a nutritional routine, choosing an unfamiliar subject to change a study routine, moving the furniture around in a room to change a view routine, changing a job status to change a work routine, getting married to change a life style routine, having a child to change a relationship routine, or a million other things. I keep practicing derailing "hypnotic" routines until it becomes a natural harmonious spontaneity for me and my loved ones. Remember God is everywhere. He is never limited to a specific routine to produce a certain blessing or miracle. He creates life out of anything, anytime and anywhere for anyone *unconditionally*. And we're made in His/That Likeness.

In my moments of doubt, I reach out into believing God *Can Change My Life*; even though I have no clue how He will. I can ask Him to give me the faith and the will to believe, ***My Life Can Change!*** Author: Optimum Vizhan. Publisher: Trafford Publishing.

Finding Christ in the Midst

This book offers us a variety of constructive inspirationals that give our hearts another chance to embrace the possibilities of our lives changing for the better. If by chance a desired change manifests, we will be living a more enriching life in a more honorable way.

Now that we have our minds and hearts are set on welcoming the idea of seeing, feeling and accepting this new change will manifest in our lives; we need to know what will be the catalyst that will cause these positive changes take place in our lives. This sequel to the book *Can My Life Change* will show us, what this life changing catalyst is and how it works. For those of us who are desperately hungry for a change in our lives, here is a juicy sneak peek preview of what this catalyst is, in conjunction to this book *Finding Christ in the Midst...*

Can the depth, width and density of *Finding Christ in the Midst* ***of My Life Changing for the Good; Multiply Exponentially so that I can feel it; on, in, with, through and around My Spirit... Feel it on, in, with, through and around My Soul... Feel it on, in, with, through and around My Body and All the Seasons of My Life... Now***

and Forevermore! Author: Optimum Vizhan. Publisher: Trafford Publishing.

Note: At the time of this publishing of Hell and Back these book titles may or may not be available to the general public. Periodically keep checking for additional books authored by Optimum Vizhan. Publisher Trafford Publishing.

Products Related to the Hell and Back Survival Tips and recommended additional books to read are available on Zazzle[R].Com at the WarriorsCreed Store. If not pending time and resources will be available at a later date. Please check back periodically.

☦ Index ☦

Printed in the United States
By Bookmasters